Orkney and the Sea

an oral history

Edited and compiled by Kate Towsey

Volunteers:
Alexander Annal
Ellen Casey
Helen Chalmers
Jenny Ireland
Calum Robertson
Scott Sutherland
Helga Tulloch
Scott Tulloch

An Orkney Heritage publication
funded by The Millennium Lottery Fund 2002

Published by
Orkney Heritage

Typeset by
Kate Towsey

Designed and Printed at
The Orcadian Limited, Hatston, Kirkwall, Orkney

ISBN 0-9540320-3-9

Sponsors
Orkney Heritage
Millennium Lottery Commission

Within his little kingdom
Beside the Birsay shore
He's tilled his few green acres
For thirty years or more,
Yet even at this farm-work
He listens to the roar
Of great Atlantic breakers,
And wanders back and fore
With eye upon the weather
Until the gods restore
The longed-for hours of sea work,
Handling creel and oar.

He's ready every evening,
Cuithe wands at the door,
Returning nigh on midnight
With ten to twenty score,
And lythe, perhaps, from Marwick
To salt and lay in store.
Thus Willie, for a lifetime
Skilled in country lore,
Has ruled his little kingdom
Beside the Birsay shore.

The Happy Fisherman, Robert Rendall

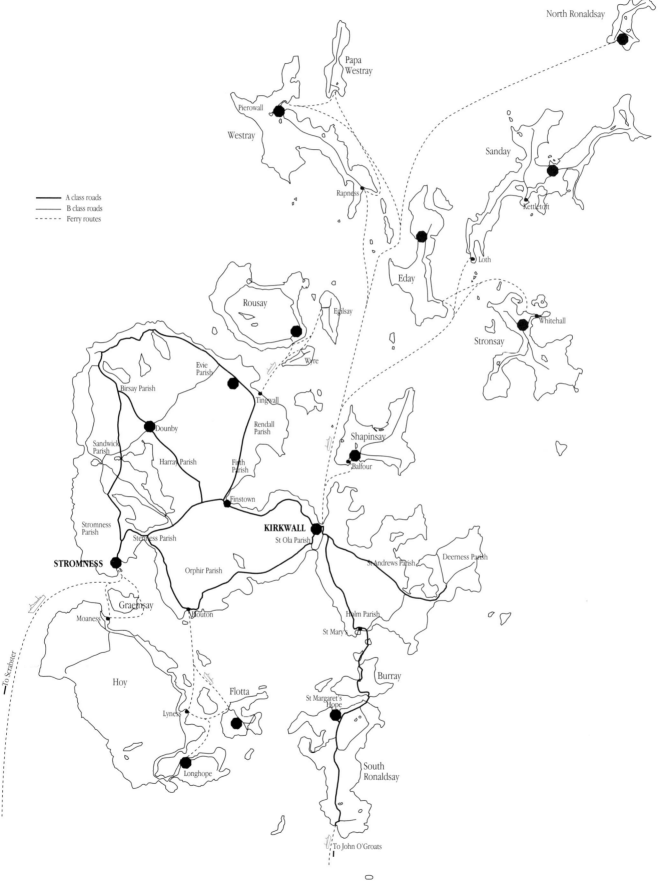

North Ronaldsay

Papa
Westray

Pierowall

Westray

Sanday

Rapness

Kettletoft

A class roads
B class roads
Ferry routes

Eday

Loth

Rousay

Egilsay

Whitehall

Evie
Parish

Stronsay

Birsay Parish

Wyre

Tingwall

Dounby

Rendall
Parish

Shapinsay

Sandwick
Parish

Harray Parish

Firth
Parish

Balfour

Finstown

KIRKWALL

Stromness
Parish

St Ola Parish

Stenness Parish

St Andrews Parish

Deerness Parish

STROMNESS

Orphir Parish

Graemsay

Houton

Holm Parish

Moaness

St Mary's

To Scrabster

Hoy

Flotta

Burray

Lyness

St Margaret's
Hope

Longhope

South
Ronaldsay

To John O'Groats

Contents

A note on the transcriptions

The words in this book have been transcribed from oral history interviews. The original recordings can be listened to through Orkney Sound Archive at Kirkwall Library, if the interviewees have given their permission for public access. The transcriptions represent a verbatim account of the recording, although it was decided not to attempt to write in dialect, mostly because of the great variety of the dialect spoken by interviewees and interviewers. In some places there have been words or phrases missed out of the transcription to aid clarity. This is indicated by three dots in the text. Similarly, where the editor has included words not on the recording to aid clarity, this is indicated by square brackets. It is impossible to represent spoken word accurately in text but every attempt has been made to remain true to the original meaning of the words spoken. In some cases, the name of a the place is added to the individual's name. This is done only where it is relevant to the content of the quote. It does not necessarily mean that that was where the individual was born or lives.

Acknowledgments

Many people have supported this project over the past two years. Some offered their time to look after volunteers travelling to the isles, some offered photographs or information, others have read through the text giving guidance and advice, without which this project would not have been possible. Thanks must go to Jim Sinclair, Bill Miller, Tony Trickett, Dru Kendall and Diana Schofield for looking after the volunteers on their travels. Bryce Wilson, Tom Muir, Anne Brundle and Steve Callaghan from Orkney Heritage all provided information and support to the volunteers and myself. Jim Purvis, Alan Cogle, Albert Scott, Louise Scott, Andrea Watt, Diane Bain, Len Wilson, Dennis Davidson, Evelyn Gunn and Jon Humphreys provided advice, photographs and information. Thank you to Elizabeth Gilmore for her excellent proof-reading skills. Thank you to Philip Astley, Colin Rendall, David Mackie and Bobby Leslie of Orkney Archives and Library for their patience in responding to endless enquiries. Thank you to BBC Radio Orkney for permission to use extracts from two of their recordings and Geoffrey Stell of the Royal Commission for Ancient and Historical Monuments for permission to use an extract from their archives and, finally, thank you to Robert P. Rendall for permission to use poems of his uncle, Robert Rendall.

Introduction

In recent years, there has been a recognition by the heritage community in Orkney, led by the museums service of the local authority, that the story of boats and boatbuilding in Orkney was fast disappearing, together with the historic boats themselves. This led to the incorporation of Orkney Boat Museum, a company with the long-term aim of establishing a museum on this subject. The local authority intends to retain ownership of its large and growing collection of boats and related artefacts, with Orkney Boat Museum displaying and interpreting the collection through a legal service agreement. With nearly 30 boats currently in the collection, and many more promised once there is a museum in place, this should be a major visitor attraction for Orkney. To find out more, or to offer artefacts or information relating to this theme, please contact the local authority museums service at museum@orkney.gov.uk, or telephone 01856 873535 and ask for The Orkney Museum.

A frequently heard description of Orcadians is 'farmers with boats' but this does no justice to the complex and ever-changing relationship people in Orkney have with the sea. Whether it is beach-combing as a child, fishing with creels or working far from home on a merchant ship, the sea is inescapable. One of the best ways of understanding this relationship is to listen to the voices of people who have lived by and from the sea.

This book is based on interviews with people in Orkney who have earned some part of their living from the sea. For most of those interviewed that has meant a lifetime of diverse occupations. The interviews were collected by Millennium volunteers from June 2000 to May 2001. Funded by the Millennium Lottery Fund, the intention of the project was to give young people between the ages of sixteen and twenty-five the opportunity to become involved in voluntary work, which would be of benefit to the community. The project benefited enormously from the enthusiasm and initiative of the young people involved.

The volunteers were given training in oral history methodology and recording technology, then went on to interview people all over Orkney. Volunteers interviewed people of all ages and backgrounds, taking photographs and recording video footage. Many discovered and developed their own research interests and made lasting friendships with those they met through the project. Many more people could have been interviewed, given the time, and many of those interviewed could have been interviewed again about different aspects of their lives. The collection will go to Orkney Library Sound Archive for the benefit of future generations where it will join the rich collection of interviews and recordings already there.

Oral history is now a respected historical tool, providing information and experiences inaccessible in other ways. The words of the people who have lived through the profound changes that they describe are as valuable as the insights of the professional historian. It would be unrealistic to say that this book represents the combined experiences gained by sixty lifetimes at sea. It provides only a sample of the wealth of knowledge accumulated, much of which would be lost without these recordings.

Inevitably there have been some subject areas omitted from the book. It was felt that, for the most part, the book should restrict itself to those earning a living from the sea, so areas like sailing and regattas have been omitted, together with recent developments such as fish farming. Orkney's wartime maritime history has also been omitted since the subject has been explored very well in a number of other publications.

CHILDHOOD

Tingwall Pier

GROWING UP BY THE SEA

The sea is irresistible to any child and, for many Orcadians growing up by the sea, childhood play on the shore and in boats gave them the beginnings of the experience needed for a lifelong relationship with the sea.

I was taken over to be baptised in Flotta … I would have been four or five months and, because it was a very dry spring and summer there was no water in the spring at the well near the Kirk. My father went down to the shore and he filled the baptismal bowl with salt water. So I was baptised with salt water … He told me that before he died.

Willie Groat, Longhope

We had a slipway and a ten and a half foot dinghy, MacKay built, and at that time it was a pound a foot. We had a ten and a half foot dinghy and that was ten pounds, ten shillings. That was with the oars and rowlocks thrown in … It was built for us … It was a grand rowing boat and we went out to the west shore, to the sillocks. Kathleen, my younger sister, was daft on coming with me and we had lots of sillocks and cuithes. We used to go out to Hoy Sound with the last of the ebb and come back with the flood and we just knew every rock … You didn't do anything foolish. You didn't go out unless the weather was convenient and the tides were suitable. The tide in Hoy Sound is too strong to row against so you need to be careful what you were doing. *Walter Leask, Stromness*

We were in boats before we could walk. *Robbie Sutherland*

We had a motor boat, a sailing boat, canoe and a flattie. My father was very generous and let youngsters have the use of the flattie provided he considered they would be safe.

In the flattie we'd row out and get the sensation of the wave of the *St Ola* coming in or we'd go out to the harbour entrance with a southerly wind, hoist our sacky sail and just sail down the harbour. Then we would graduate to third hand in the small sailing boat to bail her out or as ballast. Later we would graduate to the jib sheet and, by the time we were maybe fourteen, we'd be in charge of the boat. I learnt principles that I didn't understand [at the time]. We imitated people who could do the job…

Once I took our sailing boat out with my cousin and friends across to the lighthouse to Graemsay to see the lighthouse. When we left, having seen the lighthouse, the wind had eased considerably and the tide was ebbing, (going out the Sound) it was pointing further and further up the wind but we weren't making enough headway and the tide was stronger and having a greater effect than our sail. Therefore I got the oars out and landed in by the beacon. In Stromness there was always someone by the piers here, so someone saw my plight and they came out with a boat called the *Steinvora* and I had got them ashore but I kept the boat afloat. I couldn't possibly leave the boat there so I got them away ashore. I stayed with the boat and kept her afloat as the tide was ebbing and this boat came in and I managed to get a line to it. The tide was so strong that we couldn't go against the tide, we had to go away over the Graemsay side because the tide was weaker. So you see, these were things that we were picking up as young lads that were going to be of great use later in life.

Robbie Sutherland, Stromness

Stromness

All the piers there was old men down there and if they saw us making a mistake we got a scolding when we came in and got told we were damn stupid. They were the boys that made sure we behaved ourselves sensibly in the boat … You knew you were under observation all the time. There was a genuine desire to gain a skill. *Robbie Sutherland*

There was always fishing boats coming in – it was Inverness or Buckie fishing boats that came in – and they would be gutting the fish on the pier. Many a time they'd go and say 'get me a packet of cigarettes and a bottle of lemonade'. They would give you money and off you'd go and for that they would give you six or seven haddock.

Willie Tulloch, Stromness

A small boat called the *Wharrie Glen* came up and they were involved in carting the wheat ashore … we used to have fun when the men came ashore and the men went to the pub. A number of us young blokes would lie around one end of the store and watch them disappear up the pier. They had a hand winch and we used to have great fun winding each other aboard the boat and generally messing around with the derrick. I suppose the crew knew what we were doing but we werenae doing any harm so we got away with it … The pier was a great place, there was always something going on. At the weekend when the *Thorfinn* was in (the *Thorfinn* was in every weekend) and we just lay doon about there. I used to be friendly with all the blokes on the boat. There was a Mate on board, from Aberdeen and he was very good. He used to teach me Morse and various knots and splicing and things like that. I learnt a lot of seamanship from him. *Harcus Scott, Westray*

I used to enjoy looking at the yoles … just the shape of them, beautiful boats, fishermen had them. I always said one day I would acquire one of them and I did.

Willie Tulloch

It was always the end of March and there'd be this thud, thud, thud … The reason they had that thud was they had one cylinder engines and I'd see me sitting in school hearing these engines and you couldn't wait to get down to the pier and see these boats. *Willie Tulloch*

We played by the sea the whole time … We had a twelve foot dinghy with sails on it and played the whole summer. We had a big drouger … we'd a sail on that and we played on the beach and the sea. We had a lot of fun in it. You couldn't sink it or tip it or anything like that. … We hadn't to go by Hunda, we could go to St. Margaret's Hope or across to South Ronaldsay … there was quite a few boys had dinghies with sails and we used to do that the whole summer … me father and me grandfather taught us and then we were on our own. They rigged it up for us, to show us to begin with us. Me father and grandfather was always keen to go out fishing. Any excuse to get off and fish.

Anthony Duncan, Burray

Rousay Pier

Stromness

Michael and Jordan Thomson leaving Kirkwall Harbour

Photo: Kate Towsey

We had a whole lot of old boats and we just used to spend the whole summer holidays in boats. There was nothing else to do in old boats but go between the west shore and the Barrier.
Robin Duncan, Burray

One day in particular, I remember, we came over to Stronsay and word came down to the pier that all the meal was ready from the mill and he thought … if he could get all the men started working in the afternoon … it would save time and he put me and my brother aboard the boat. We couldn't start the engine, he started the engine for us and sent us across [from Stronsay to Papa Stronsay]. I would have been seven or eight, my brother would have been maybe six and he said, after the boat left for Papay, if the boat went on fire [he could have done] nothing. I think he got a ticking-off from me mother that night.

We had a wee dinghy that we were starting to go in and [my father] got worried and sold the dinghy, much to our disgust … I think he was a bit worried we might go overboard. It certainly gave me an awful taste for boats. My father didn't think I would stay on the farm. He was sure I would go to sea but, when I came to the age to go, I felt that my parents were well on and they would need me home to help on the farm … but we weren't long in Westray before we had a boat, took up sailing.
Jack Scott

Later on he used to take us round the shore. He would go to the creels and he could drop us off at any of the little geos and we could just run home, so we must have been going from when we were quite young, just for a little treat. Obviously we wanted to go. I've never been afraid of the water.

Very occasionally you would be allowed to take the tiller. You felt so big and in control of the boat, little did you know that he had checked everything out. The only time he let us do anything was when we were out fishing for pilticks, that's greyfish. We didn't have any fancy fishing rods, we just had a line we dropped over the side of the boat.
Helen Manson, South Ronaldsay

It has been said that fishermen in particular do not want to learn to swim, that, if they should fall into the water, they would prefer to drown quickly. It is more probable that unsafe beaches, cold water and custom were the main reasons that so many Orcadians never learnt to swim. Stromness swimming pool was built in 1969 with money raised from public subscription. Since then Kirkwall and many of the islands have had pools built.

We had a disaster here when two boys drowned. They were sailing in a boat that was a wee bit less stable than the others. With a westerly wind, the strength can be deceiving as gusts, which we called swaps, sweep down from the Brinkies or Hellihole and can be sighted as dark areas on top of the sea. Certain areas where this took place were well known by those who regularly sailed the boats. The strength of the wind had to be taken into account when westerly wind prevailed. *Robbie Sutherland, Stromness*

We could swim like fish. We was in the sea the whole time. Three, four times a day I've seen us swimming in the summertime. The sea didna have much fear for us. I mean, you treated the sea with respect, you've got to do that, but we were good swimmers. *Anthony Duncan*

I learnt to swim by my own efforts … nobody could swim in them days … It was very cold water and there was no swimming pool … We used to swim about the rocks … A lot of people in the Isles can swim now because I fought hard for a swimming pool … a lot of the Westray boys are fishermen nowadays and I know of a fella who fell overboard at the pier and because nobody heard him, he drowned and he was just no distance from the beach. He could have swum. The womenfolk thought it was high time that they were learning to swim. *Jack Scott*

I could not swim. None of the people, nobody at the school, nobody that I know of, could swim. The excuse was that there was no sandy beach or safe place. We were told it was not safe to go in the water …. Never entered our head when we got into a boat. We never thought that being able to swim would have saved us …

When my children were quite young I had made up me mind that they should know how to swim … I never thought I would go along with them, I just thought it was very important that children should be able to swim. I used to take them down to beside the Barrier in Burray, for it was nice and warm there, it was flat, there was no danger. We would take them down there and this lady would come out from Kirkwall and she taught them. *Helen Manson*

We were dooked, we would doggy paddle. We'd jump off the pier and then doggy paddle in to the ladder. We couldn't swim properly. This crane that's on the end of the pier here was used to swing out and then drop into the sea. During the school time the many of the boys and girls would swim from the piers, slipways or lifeboat slip. We knew that during rain the sea was slightly warmer so when it was raining, as long as we had a shed to leave our clothes, we would be in the water at dinnertime …

Rousay bairns going home from the Kirkwall school hostel for the weekend on the *Orna* in the 1960s

Pierowall, Westray

A brother of mine capsized the boat here and he couldn't
swim ... They had a lifebelt in the boat but ... within
a couple of weeks he swam the harbour. He found that
swimming was valuable.
                                    Robbie Sutherland

Gutting fish, Stromness

Photo: Orkney Library, Photographic Archive

Photo: Orkney Library, Photographic Archive

SHORE

Tangles on the pier, Eday

SEAWEED

The shoreline was as important to the livelihood of Orkney people as the sea itself. All but two Orkney parishes have a shoreline and those parishes have access rights to the shores of other parishes. For some purposes the shorelines were communally accessible, at other times they were carefully divided up between households when tangles or seaweed were gathered.

Kelp

The kelp industry is almost beyond the reach of living memory. Kelp started to be processed in Orkney in the eighteenth century when it was used as a source of alkali for the glass and soap industries. Tangles were gathered by hand and, where possible, piled on a cart to be taken to the steethe where they were dried. Kelp was later valued as a source of iodine. Kelp burning died out in the 1930s.

I can just remember it being done. At the time when the pits were burning you couldn't see anything, just a dense fog of the kelp reek up from the pits. I just remember the tail end of it. Then the last of it was stored for years in the old kelp store but eventually in the wartime it was shipped off. I would only have been nine or ten …

John Cutt, North Ronaldsay

Photo: Orkney Library, Photographic Archive

Eday

They used to go to the Aikerness Holm, see the wee house in the middle, that's where they used to stay. Four or five of them stayed in that house in the middle all week and came home at the weekends. My great-grandfather and his brother were two of the ones that used to do it and he used to tell us about it and they had this two-wheeled barrow that they worked wi' and when the wind was in the right direction they hoisted a sail on it, the sail of the boat to help them up the beach with the tangles. Then they burnt it and put it in bags and then a big boat used to come and they beached her and filled her with the kelp and then waited for tide to come in and take her away.

Thomas D. Rendall

I gied with some food if they were going to be doon there a while … it's a different smell from wood or coal burning.

Jenny Tulloch, North Ronaldsay

I remember the pits being burnt and you had what is known as the kelp rake … a long bit o'iron with a wooden handle because when it was hot it was just molten and it was very hot, a beautiful substance …   *Geordie Costie, Westray*

Tangles

Since the Second World War people, mainly in Westray and North Ronaldsay, have earned money by collecting and drying tangles. The tangles were originally processed to make alginates, which have a diverse range of applications. The tangles were collected and then stacked on racks to dry over winter. They were then tied together in bundles, taken to the pier where they were picked up and taken to a processing plant in Uist. The work was never sufficiently well-paid to provide a sole income and has only ever been a supplement to a family income. The last tangles were collected in Orkney in 1999. The industry now uses Chilean tangles, which lose more moisture when air dried. There is potential for using this resource in the future; it is now possible to harvest tangles, not just collect them from the shore.

Every township had its own area of the shore for tangles ... it divided up where there was a lot of tangles taken up. You might only have for your share, then less favourable places you would have more but each one was equal. Every household has its share ... everyone was down there when it was gathered and someone paced it out and there was a few stones put up, divided between one and another ... it was your tangle 'mates'. Every small bit of the shore had its name ...   *John Cutt*

It's never cold when you're gathering, your hands are never cold when you're gathering, see when you're putting them on the pile, that's the time when your hands get cold. When they've lain up in the air a long time but when they've been in the sea your hands never got cold.

You just had your own sort of beach ... the boat came early in July. Everybody had their beach that they worked on ... In later years work was very few. Now it's all history. It was all just done by tractor ... everybody just took their own to the pier ... In the end we got a hundred and seventy-six pounds a dry ton ... Maybe when collecting was at its best you would take two or three days to collect a ton ... In the wintertime you would spend all the daylight hours at it. You just needed time ... It was a good healthy job. It was tiring, hard work and heavy work. There are just certain parts of the island where it comes ashore, but it was a very good thing for the islands.

I worked there before I went to Glasgow, the fifties. At that time they were nine pounds a ton and when I came back it was a one hundred and seventy pounds a ton ... There was an awful lot went out of Westray at that time ... I used to have the job of going round weighing them and working out the carting. It took weeks to do it. We weighed the whole thing with a scale on three legs, a spring with a platform on it and you laid every bundle on it. It was some work ... The last tangles was just a case of going with your cart onto the weighbridge.   *Thomas D. Rendall*

They worked down in the tangles, usually before the lighthouse went out in the morning and it was always lighted at night before we came home, all winter. It was hard.

In the old days there was some families that had very little and they would go out in the morning and not come back until the evening.

Did they take food with them?

Well they had no food to bring, if they were big families.

Everyone went to the tangles. Every day, yes, if there were tangles. Then you had to stack them. The tangle stacks would be at Bride's Kirk, that was a good beach for tangles. And you only had four places to stack. The stacks would be as high as you could put one tangle on the top, standing on a fish box.

I can remember it would have been started in the mid-fifties. It was good money when there was nothing. It is a hard job but latterly we had winches and then there was tractors and link boxes so that took the really hard work out of it. It used to be all thrown. There was some people who would manage to put up twenty tons of dried tangles in a winter, just by throwing, on their own.   *John Cutt*

... stones were just built on a hill at the top of the beach where your share was ... you could spend the whole day, every day but it depended on the tide of course. Weather, it made no difference. We only could get them up from the sea when it was ebb tide then they had to be stacked after. If the tide came in you could start stacking ...   *Oliver Scott*

Fertiliser

Ware is the name given to all weeds found exposed at the lowest tides and the permanently submerged beds of seaweed. Storms drive the weed to the shore. It was found most plentifully on the eastern shores of the islands. Traditionally it was laboriously carted up the beach and piled to rot into the soil and fertilise the crops.

Ware is the traditional Orkney fertiliser, still used today by organic farmers and gardeners. It has been described by William Thomson as 'the most important of the beach resources. The cold, laborious work of carrying up seaweed and spreading it on the land was familiar to generations of farmers and cottars. It was the means by which the fertility of the land was sustained by alternate cropping with oats and bere with no period of fallow'.

Thomson, W.P.L., Kelp-Making in Orkney, p.16

In the first break in the wintertime stuff called tang came in and he threw that on next year's tattie land it was good land ... they always thought they had a better crop if they had tang on the ground.   *Jack Scott*

It was completely different for the ware. You got bigger shares dependent on the size of your croft ... it was divided in halves to start with, one section of the township divided the halves and the other side of the township picked whatever half they wanted and it went like that. One person divided and the other person picked the section. There was no cheating, you couldn't cheat.   *Oliver Scott*

Sarah of Hooking spreading ware, North Ronaldsay, 1933

At very low tides you would get a dulse, like a vegetable, sweet and it was lovely to chew ... we carted seaweed up to the land and that was our winter programme, spreading the seaweed on the land very evenly and then it was ploughed in. You used to have to walk along with the plough to keep the couter, that cut the farrow, you'd to keep it clear otherwise it would gather up. So we had a stick and we would keep it clear.   *Willie Groat, Longhope*

It was divided between the different houses ... It was the menfolk that parted it, that divided it into sections ... the area covered. They divided it as equally as they could, then they drew lots, usually stones, so you had to take your pick.

First of all it was put in little heaps then it was spread all over the field ... It was only in the springtime that you carted the ware. It was only in the springtime that ware was available, it was just washed ashore ... it was used as a fertiliser because there was no artificial fertiliser coming to the island at that time. It was ware and dung from the middens.   *Jenny Tulloch*

You had a draw-fork and you raked that up and put it up above the high water mark and that was yours. Everyone recognised their own.   *Willie Groat, Longhope*

I've seen my father cutting tang, waiting for the right direction of wind and going down with the scythe and cutting tang 'til it came ashore and putting it on the grund for the tatties.   *Thomas D. Rendall*

They had ware spades, they were very straight ... they used to cut the ware sections, to cut the ware with these spades then stick a ... hook to let you see where the cut had been made. Folk used to stick tangles up to show the sections ...   *Jenny Tulloch*

Each part of the shoreline has a special name, probably now only known to older local inhabitants and rarely written down. Thomas D. Rendall of Westray has recorded place-names he knew around the coast of Westray near where he lived at Buckleberry. It was important for many reasons to be able to name different locations precisely and these place-names illustrate some of the history behind the local community and the uses to which different parts of the coastline were put. Westray Development Trust now has a long term project recording place names all over Westray.

1. Rammy Geo

2. Cummly Geo. Named after the round boulders or cummels in it.

3. Millary Geo. Named after the pebbles or millar in it.

4. Jeemies Geo

5. Less Jock

6. Smerry Geo. Where legend has it the Vikings first landed on Westray. They ate a meal off two large rocks in the geo which are known as the tables of Smerry Geo.

7. Smacks Geo. Where a welled fishing smack was wrecked, called the *North Star*. Off the coast lies the bow. A trawler was wrecked on this in 1906 called the *Badger*. This was the first rescue by breeches buoy by the Papa Westray lifesaving team. In 1916 a Swedish coaster, the *Birka*, was lost here with the loss of all of the crew and included the Captain's wife

8. Sandy Geo

9. Giaros Geo

10. The Cummels. After the round boulders which litter the beach round here

11. Hoobacker

12. Liarco

13. Noust. Where fishing boats landed when they were creeling etc and were laid in nousts

14. Horniber

15. Sweestibacker

16. Jeemie Reid's Hole. A sandy spot on the sea bottom just off the rocks, known as the Less, where it was certain you would get a lobster in the creel. It was used by Jeemie Reid of Westbreck and named after him.

17. Geo o'Breck. Where the inhabitants of Breck were allowed to gather tangles.

18. Spenso

19. The Heid

20. The Storehouse

21. Avertaft

22. The Baars

23. The Loup o' the Ayre

24. The Ayre

25. The Fluck Pow

26. The Black Rocks

27. The Ause

28. Mollievenier

29. Sweenkhole or Blowhole. A blowhole about twenty yards from the cliff. Originally this was open and the water swilled around or 'sweenkled' in it. A boy who was herding sheep fell in and was lost, with his dog. Iron bars were placed across it and stones were placed over it. Because of the partial blockage by the stones, when a heavy sea runs it blows and makes a loud noise.

30. The Neeming Stone. The neeming stone or steen where it was customary to carve your initials

31. Vavals Geo – The Geo where Archie Angell came ashore.

32. Hau

33. Stave

34. Bendibar

35. Dicks Geo

36. Whinber

Kelp burning p

'. The Miss Skerries

. The Quoydyke

. Dirt Hole

The Bout. Bout was a word used for a pen into which sheep were driven for catching.

The Craig Bouts

The Shepherd's House. Where at one time there was a small hut in which the shepherd of Skaill sheltered and took his piece.

The Shelly Holm

Davies Less

The Less of Noust

The Less

Soweless

The Kelp Green. The place where ware could be spread out and dried before being burnt in the kelp pits

Punding, North Ronaldsay, 2000

SHEEP

North Ronaldsay is now well-known for the unique breed of sheep which survives on the shore of the island, eating mainly seaweed. They are not communally owned but getting the animals together is, by necessity, a community task where everyone on the island is needed to guide the sheep into punds for clipping etc. The sheep are kept on the shore for most of the year, separated from the farmland by a dyke.

They have certain areas, what we call 'clow gung'* and mother of course, you see was from that area. The lamb follows the mother and they don't want to move from that restricted area where they can get to the grass and to favourite feeding grounds.

If you had a crowd of pet lambs they would have none to guide them and therefore they would stay about the dykes and the gates and not realise that they had to go down to feed … In the olden days you only put down the ewes to the shore when there was a spring tide coming on, not when there was plenty of feed on the shore so that the others trained the lamb to go down to begin with and they would be a bit hungry after the day or two and there would be the main tide and they would go down and there would be plenty to eat. The lamb got trained then to follow its mother's habits.

The punds at the north end were put in on New Year's Eve and New Year's Day. That was a tradition because of taking the sheep out for slaughter at that time … they are not like conventional sheep because they are in their best condition around Christmas time … the seaweed loses its nutritional value in spring … That's where the practice started of bringing the ewes in to grass in the springtime because they can't [eat enough for their needs]. The sheep used to roam about all over the place once the crop was in. There was holes in the dyke for that very purpose [in the days before rye grasses were sown].

There's a little over two thousand two hundred sheep … there's over twelve miles of sheep dyke. For the privilege of every sheep we have the obligation to maintain about ten yards of dyke. Although in one way we have them free, we have the privilege but we also have the obligation.

I've seen them getting impatient, at an ebb tide. I've seen them swimming to a favourite bit of rock but the experienced ones don't get caught out. *John Cutt*

The women didn't go to the punds in my young days. It was just the menfolk but there was plenty of men you see. *Jenny Tulloch*

There used to be, where we now use wire to block them, in the past it used to be a whole line of people that did that and you used to see hundreds of sheep coming at you and it was really quite exciting and you had to physically stop them which could be quite dangerous for small, young folk because the sheep would jump over them or into them.

My father used to talk about teams of people, criers, that would chase the sheep … so many would do a certain distance and then a fresh group would take over and there might be three or four groups of people that would keep the sheep on the move. That's the thing with punding is to keep them moving. If you give them time to come back or to think, you'll have problems because they can break away in the wrong direction entirely. In fact they make a practice of that but if you keep them moving all the time they don't have time to think so it is still important, the crying part of it, but we have the hurdles. *Ian Scott*

It used to be there was any number of people to hold the sheep in but now we use Shire wire. We have punds, which are stone enclosures which keep … the sheep together [so that they can be handled].

Of course, it's regulated by the tides, the full tide with the spring means that most of the rocks are covered and there is less space for the sheep to run and you need quite a lot of people to gather the sheep because they are quite different from conventional sheep because they act on their own, independently. If one thinks it sees a way of escape then it will take it, never mind what happens to the rest. Punding takes place usually early in the New Year when the mature sheep are taken out for slaughter. In April we have a pre-lambing punding, ewes are taken into grass and in late July, August we have a clipping punding. We used to have a dipping punding in October. *John Cutt*

To get theirs in they have to help get everyone else's in so it's in everybody's interest to make it a successful pund. But it's a lightsome affair when people have a chance to talk about this and that …

On Sundays, the older sheep men it was a day for wandering around the dykes and looking … there was men from the older townships who would enjoy just going down to the beach to have a look because they had some real interest in their sheep. It wasn't for money, it was for necessity and I think people working together for necessity rather than money, there's a different attitude there, there's a different type of person. *Ian Scott*

* A particular section of the foreshore that ewes and their lambs feed from and frequent each year.

Shooting seals for sport

Skinning seals, 1960s

SEALS

Seals, locally known as selkies, have always been a strong part of Orcadian legend and story. Their aspect makes them seem almost human. Traditionally seal meat was eaten, the skins were cured and seal-oil was used in lamps and in a variety of domestic ways.

Seal-oil was very good for lots of things, a cruisie lamp. It didn't just smell very good but sometimes it was used for lighting.   *Willie Groat, Longhope*

I used to cut the blubber off and melt it in a big bin wi' a big fire underneath it and it was used to put on machinery and to mix wi' paint for painting. It is the very best for machinery. Certain machinery … one man put it in the chamber o' his baler and it was a mistake. When he gies to bale wi' it on his baler and it nearly burst his baler for it goes on thick … A lot of folk used to mix it with paint, it put a good coat on it …

Was it used for waterproofing boots?

I've never done that. It has a terrible smell, you wouldn't be allowed in the house with it if you put it on your boots for if you came near a fire it would be very strong, an oily smell.

When I came home from the whaling a sealskin was five pounds and if you worked the whole week on a farm you might have got seven pounds so there wereny much choice for me.   *Marcus Hewison, Westray*

I can remember my father having seal-oil in the hoose and every year when they finished ploughing they coated it with seal-oil. It dried like varnish you know. It was great for keeping the rust off.   *Thomas D. Rendall*

Government culls took place from 1970, initiated in response to accusations that seal numbers were damaging fish stocks. The last seal cull took place in 1984-85 and seals are now protected. No licences to shoot seals have been issued since 1988. Killing of seals has recently aroused strong passions and, in the 1970s, they became the focus for animal rights protestors. There have been accusations of seals attacking lobster creels and salmon farms, endangering livelihoods. There have also been rarely-solved instances of illegal seal culling.

I used to hunt seals when I was younger. Heavy, hard, dirty work. I wouldn't want to go back to it for nothing. It was good money, that's why we went to it.

To me seals are like any natural resource, you farm them. You take some but leave plenty.   *Geordie Costie, Westray*

I hunted seals for years. A lot of years, shot five hundred a year. That's when I had a licence for it. In Westray and all o'er there were so many. We were shooting five hundred and it was no problem to get five hundred. Now there were ten thousand pups on Faray island last year … more and more every year … They were just farmed like any other and it just kept the numbers right. But noo there are too many … You see far more with disease … they are so over-populated. There are so many in one piece they can't move hardly.

The skins gied doon to London, for I suppose to make things with, then you got as much as ten pounds top price for a skin, we were very glad o' it at that time … that was a great source of income … Just walking the shore. They are white when they are pups and they stay a month on the shore and then they change to silver-grey coats … and that is when they are harvested, they are shot when they are changed ready to go to sea. They are just shot on land. It's all humanely done … It's hard work. Sometimes you had to carry them on your back for a piece … you had them all to pull down out into dinghies then them all to put in the big boat, a lot of lifting, oh it was hard work. Sometimes you couldna land on one side and you had to carry them on your back to the other side. It wasna easy but you had to do it, it was your living.

They had special knives for it, the knives was just curved, and you just skinned them and then they were washed in heat water, then cold water and heat water again … in salty water … then they were just dyed and just salted and folded edge to edge and rolled up and when they were salted, then they'd keep as long as you want …   *Marcus Hewison*

Then the greenies, the likes of Greenpeace were protesting so much … they were throwing stones through the windows of people who sold the seal products so that totally destroyed the markets but I have discovered nowadays how easy it is to get money for showing a tourist a seal that I am now the most reformed seal hunter you would ever come across.   *Alex Costie*

Sixteen per cent of all grey seals were born on Orkney coastlines in 1999. Parts of Sanday's coastline, Faray and the Holm of Faray are European S.A.C.s (Special Areas of Conservation). Muckle and Little Green Holm, Eynhallow as well as Ward Hill in South Ronaldsay are S.S.S.I.s (Sites of Special Scientific Interest), giving protection to common and grey seals.

A spoot tide at Echna Bay beach, Burray

Elyse and Gary Miller raking for cockles, Echna Bay beach, Burray

SHELLFISH

Archaeological evidence indicates that shellfish were an important part of the prehistoric diet and, up to the nineteenth century, shellfish provided nutrition at times when the crops failed. Today shellfish are eaten as a matter of personal preference rather than need. Whelks have been, and still are, collected for cash and still eaten as a delicacy. Cockles and spoots are eaten where people have access to the right kinds of sandy shoreline. Limpets were only used as bait or, in one exceptional case, in desperation by a lighthouse man, Jimmy Groat, and his assistant when the supply boat was ten days late. They are tough to eat and tricky to knock off a rock but at least they are easy to find. Generally shellfish are only eaten in the spring and autumn as the naturally occurring toxins are more concentrated in the summer months.

At school the Headmaster asked 'Who'd like to go catching spoots this afternoon?' and of course everyone put their hand up, whether you wanted to go or not, if you didn't, someone kicked you from the desk behind … so the Headmaster would get on his motor bike and come and show us how to do it … and he would walk backwards and, with the weight on the sand, a small bubble would appear and of course you knew there was a spoot down there and you just plunged down, this was a wooden board with a very sharp edge on it and caught the spoot … he wanted some for himself … he knew the area very well and he wasn't going to miss a spoot ebb just because he was Headmaster. *Willie Groat, Longhope*

My father was quite good at getting spoots. You watched for the spoot, a bit of water would shoot up and if you had good strong hands you can dig in and get hold of them. Springtime is a big time, when you get your big tides. *Harcus Scott*

You put them in hot water to get them off their shells then you didna need to cook them much, just briefly in the pan. If you cook them too long they go so hard you can hardly eat them. They come out tremendous. We used to get a lot in Westray, bucketfuls. *Jack Scott*

We were never allowed to eat mussels during the summertime, nobody would ever pick up a mussel, similarly whelks and that sort of thing. That's the only shellfish we had on this coastline … we were always told about this poison that was in them in the summertime. *Helen Manson*

They went to the spoots when there was a spoot ebb in March and there are spoot ebbs again in September, when the big tides were. All the people went to the spoots, all the people that were able and the men and some of the women. There were huge catches of spoots and it wasn't unusual to have a hundred spoots in one tide, or even more then if there were one or two in the family but in those days there were no refrigerators or deep freezers so they couldna keep them … they ate and ate and ate them as much as they could. Some of the men then would bait the fishing-line with them and go out round the shore … and fish whitefish. They would go off with their small lines and they caught fish … if they had a huge catch then they would maybe get a wheelbarrow and go round and sell the fish but normally it was just a small line and they just gave fish here and there to their friends. *Meg Fiddler*

Some folk used to eat whelks but I didna like them … they did eat whelks. I used to gather whelks … It was the first money that I made was gathering whelks, it was five shillings a bushel … they were sent to Danny Meil as well. I remember the first money that I made. I think I bought a pair of shoes wi' it, five shillings … It took a while to gather whelks indeed, sometimes they weren't right plentiful. *Jenny Tulloch*

Whelks were painstakingly slow, you used a darning needle to get the piece of meat out of the shell, nah … it took a long time to satisfy your appetite. *Willie Groat, Longhope*

A lot of folk ate a lot of cockles as well … and some of the small crofters ate an awful lot of cockles because they were available, they were life-savers. *Harcus Scott*

Cockles were eaten, all you did was just poured boiling water on them, and ate them just like that, just leepid, you didna cook them … practically raw. If you wanted to fry them you could. The spoots were leepid, just enough to get them open and again they were fried but they needed a very short time in the pan or they were just like leather. Usually they were eaten with floory bannocks or bere bannocks. *Harcus Scott*

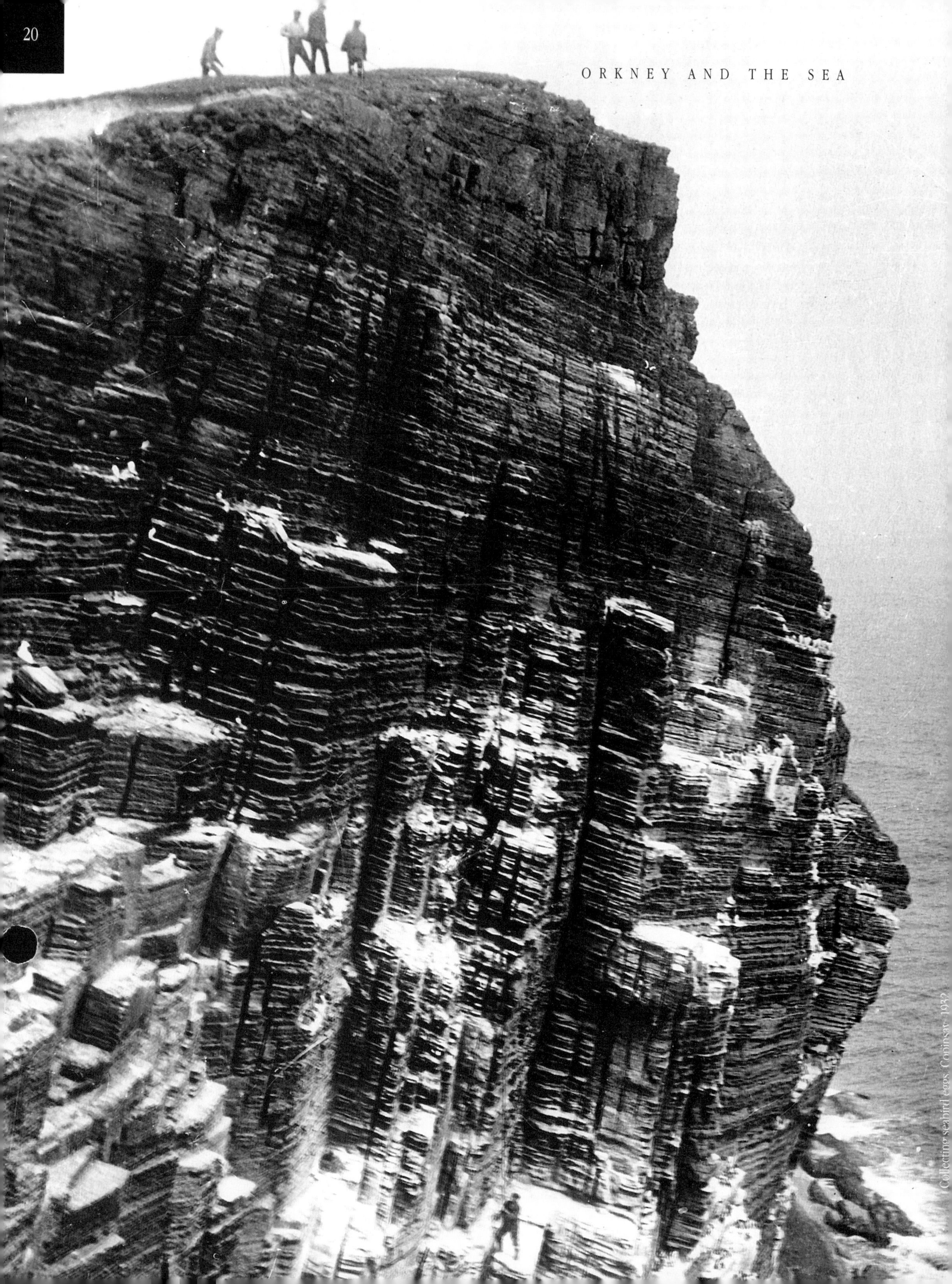

Collecting seabird eggs, Copinsay, 1932

E G G S

The eggs of wild birds were traditional fare for Orcadians. During the nineteenth century they also formed an export trade. They were gathered from the cliffs in places like Copinsay and Westray, and shipped out of Orkney. After this trade came to an end in 1914, local people still gathered wild birds' eggs, but now only for their own use. Farming was still a marginal existence in many ways and these eggs were an excellent source of nutrition, particularly at a time of year when stores for animals and humans were running low after the winter. For some, collecting the eggs was simply a case of walking over the hillsides where birds nested. Others lowered each other down the cliffs to get better access to the nests.

All kinds of eggs were tried although gulls' eggs were a favourite. These days most birds are protected and it is illegal to gather eggs, even for your own consumption.

I used to eat a lot of wild bird eggs. Any kind of wild bird egg … gull eggs … used to eat different kinds of eggs, different tastes. It's all food. *Marcus Hewison*

Before the First World War … and a lot of men in Deerness went down and they put a man down on a rope, all along the high cliffs … My father used to work at it … you never just got two the same colour, they were awfully bonny shells. *Jimmy Groat*

Gull eggs on the hill you would have them or black-head eggs, sometimes eider duck eggs … there wasn't so much feed for the animals at that time, to over-winter your cattle some of them would have been in kinda poor condition in the springtime, quite often birds' eggs from the cliffs were taken to supplement the feed … it didna do any harm, I don't think, taking the first laid eggs, for the birds would lay again. *Alex Costie*

The aaks' eggs were difficult to get. The lapwings, the first brood was always taken. They reckoned at that time that it was beneficial to the lapwing because they took the first eggs and their next litter was further into the year and the weather was better and they could survive better. There were plenty about when they were taking the eggs. *Thomas D. Rendall*

[They were] put in calves' milk. They might have skimmed milk that they were giving to the calves because they'd taken the cream off for making butter. *Alex Costie*

They used to eat a lot of wild eggs … gulls', you needed to have a taste for it because the last one I tried I couldna eat. You would just have to go over the hill. There were no wardens here then. *Willie Groat, Papa Westray*

We used to go climb for eggs, guillemot eggs, gulls' eggs. They just lay for a time, just for a month or so. We ate most of them, boiled them, salt and butter then … you see the guillemots don't make nests, just lay in the rocks and the difficulty is getting to the ledges down the cliff. We used to get two or three ropes and tie them together and take one of the boys and lower him down the cliff, a hundred feet down with another rope tied round the bucket … hanging in mid-air then he'd get to a ledge and collect up the eggs and put them in the bucket and I would pull them up then pull him up after the eggs were gathered … and go to the next bit …

One time, me and this younger brother, the gulls were starting to lay and he seen this nest down the cliff but when he got to the top he couldnae get up there was no a rock that he could grip onto and he said 'Have you got some binder twine in your pocket?' and I said 'Yes' and they were short lengths and tied them together and double it over and sent it down to him and pulled him up and he had the eggs in his bonnet. I was telling someone about it and he said 'What would have happened if the binder twine had broke?' and I said 'Oh, there's plenty more in the barn'.

They'd lay more than one if you took one away, you could come out again in a week or ten days and you could get more eggs. I've taken seven gulls' eggs out of one nest, just kept taking them to seven eggs but he went on strike after that, didn't lay any more.

There was no many puffins in Copinsay but they made burrows like rabbits. They are a small bird but they lay an egg just like a bantam egg and you put them in a bucket to see if they were fresh and if they were then you'd boil them, just like a hen's egg. *Jimmy Groat, Copinsay*

William Wilson, wild-fowler

F O W L I N G

In a similar tradition to gathering eggs, sea birds were caught for the pot. Wildfowlers 'swapped' birds on the cliffs with nets fixed to long poles, a tradition similar to Shetland and Faroe. There has never been any trade in wild bird flesh but they were commonly eaten until it became illegal to shoot wild birds. The days of 'swapping' birds have now passed from living memory as people were more likely to be shooting birds either from the shore or from a fishing boat.

We used to eat eider ducks more than guillemots because there were more eider ducks in our area than guillemots I would say … and cormorants was better still, especially the brown ones, the juvenile ones. The meat in that is tender, better than any of the other birds I would say, apart from curlews I would say but nobody seems to eat that sort of thing nowadays. They are just dying of old age and going to waste.

Alex Costie

My grandmother came off a croft in the north end … och it was just the poorest of the land they were on and everything had to go into the pot. They lived just mostly off what he shot or caught.

Thomas D. Rendall

We were gan up to that guillemot cliff and just shot them … They would just be sitting in the cliffs and when you shot them they just fell into the sea and you just picked them up … When we was younger we took the whole thing home and me mother or me grandmother would skin them … They sometimes left them in water over night, soaking them, you know it is very dark coloured flesh that's in them … sometimes they were just stewed but usually they were just boiled, you know boiled until the flesh fell off the bones, fried up with onions …

The guillemots that came here, they still come here … you'll no get any more here unless you build more cliffs because the cliffs are full of them … It was always a great source of food for the old folk, you see. No expense, you didna have any vet's bills or anything … and the guillemot is quite a hefty bird.

Alex Costie

Pretty strong, a dunter, there is nothing wrong with a dunter, they are kinda ducky tasting, but scarfs, you need a good lot of onions fried up with them in the pan. Aaks, they were good.

Thomas D. Rendall

I like them, different kinds of birds. We used to call them aaks. I don't know what their right name would be. They have been hunted for years … they are very good. I used to live on them, used to shoot them and eat them … the aaks, you shoot them when you are out on the boat. You shoot them and they fall in the sea and you pick them up and eat them, except the cormorants. Sometimes if they are coming into land and the wind is right you can shoot them from the land but otherwise you can shoot them off the boat.

I skinned them coming home in the boat, washed them in sea water, then put them to steep in salt water for a day or two. Boiled them, then fried them, wi' onions. It was very good … some birds you can pluck them but no wild birds …

We always had fresh ones to ourselves and salted ones for the winter then dried them on top of the roof then took them in and hung them up for wintertime.

Marcus Hewison

MAKING A LIVING

Placing lobsters in the kist, Stroma

CREELING

At the start of the twentieth century many Orcadians had some experience of working creels. It was an activity which complemented other kinds of work. It was conducted inshore after a day's work from around April until harvest time. It wasn't just farmers who kept creels; it was seen as a useful way of supplementing any income. Often a father would work with a child or neighbours would work side by side. Occasionally husband and wife would work together. Lobsters were caught then sent on to Danny Meil's in Kirkwall or, later, Orkney Fishermen's Society in Stromness, from where they were sent off to markets in Aberdeen and London. Some, from South Ronaldsay, got taken across the Firth to John O'Groats then to Thurso and the train to London and Billingsgate.

Photo: Orkney Library, Photographic Archive

James Wilson hauling creels at the Lash, Graemsay, 1950s

My father owned this boat and he went with this neighbour … they were really great friends, something he enjoyed as well, he loved the sea so it was no great hassle to go to the lobsters.
Helen Manson, South Ronaldsay

It was quick made money, that was the beauty of it. Whereas, if you were working on other kinds of work, you had to wait for your money.
Willie Mowatt, South Ronaldsay

I went to the lobster fishing with [my father] part of one summer. It was lovely going out on a summer morning … the water was smooth and the summer seemed to be better then … I used to row the boat and he hauled the creels …

I loved the fishing. It's a grand healthy life. Up in the morning and early away. It's grand. The smell o'the sea, a creel coming in with a lobster flopping, the tail banging about, it is a grand sound, a grand sight. I loved the fishing but it just got the way that it wasna worthwhile.

Marcus Hewison, Westray

It was all along the shore, that's when the lobsters werenae very plentiful, except in the harvest time, that's when they migrated. You would maybe get five or six, out of fifty creels, they were shipped off every fortnight to Danny Meil. It was very little.
Jenny Tulloch, North Ronaldsay

He had about a hundred [creels], all pulled by hand. We went out about half past five at night and came in about half past nine at night. We did it as long as it was weather, in the summer. We didn't go out in the wintertime. It was just summertime, up until this time of year [September] we had no lights on the boat.

There were six or seven small boats [working from Burray]. Grandfather's boat would have been the biggest at twenty-four feet, the rest of them would have been about eighteen feet, again all just one-man boats … A lot of them were just part-timers. John Wylie was the baker and he was finished about lunchtime and he went out to the creels in the afternoon or evening … There was no one who went to them full-time … . Nobody had a creel-hauler in those days, it was all single creels. And it wasn't the nice, soft rope, it was that rough coir, you know like the doormat, no rubber gloves either … I usually fished for bait, mackerel. You either fished for a bit on your way out or on the way back. Of course we only worked Saturday morning in the workshop which meant you had Saturday afternoon to fish for bait and of course you salted the bait down. Nobody had fridges or freezers, you just salted them doon in barrels.
Robin Duncan, Burray

Photo: Orkney Library, Photographic Archive

At the creels, off Hoy

I had about thirty creels I worked myself, kept me going in pocket money ... I had the wee yole and used that all around the shore. I worked on it myself, it was my wee bit of sideline ... I made the creels and weighed down with a stone, a stone fixed in the middle of the creel which sank them, which kept it where you planted it and a long line up to the surface with some corks on it so you could see it. Some folk painted them red, some painted them white so you knew your own creels from your neighbour ... there was the main frame holding the net out, a wooden bottom, a stone fixed in the middle and a big wire bent into a loop made on the creel and two holes to let the lobster get in. There was a ring and a hole ... a trap so they could get in but not get out again ... a lot of folk baited them with mackerel in they days but I used to work wi' cuithes and the backs of old partans, what bits we didna used to eat ... I pulled the creels every day ... Out of five or four creels you'd get a lobster. *Jimmy Groat*

Depended entirely on the weather ... If a suitable tide was early we had to go early ... you had to judge the area and the wind direction ... If the wind was too strong you had to call it all off, finish for the day ... it was pretty hard work ... if it was a fine day it was right enjoyable. I think the most enjoyable thing about lobster fishing was working close inshore, just around the rocks ... in a fathom of water or so ... that took a lot of the labour out ... sometimes you were very lucky fishing inshore. Eventually we got up to ... something like fifteen to seventeen fathoms ... that's hauling by hand, but we had the creels designed so that they came up on end ... which took the strain off ... At first when we started to work outside we had a lot of luck ... the grounds had never been fished; ever. This was before the seine netters started here, we found certain spots where there were very high numbers of lobsters ... but it didn't last long once the seine net boats got on the sea ... they came from Shetland ... they got some very heavy catches ... behind the reef dyke in the deep water ... they were working in twenty fathom or more ... In the end the deep water fishing was more or less finished. Numbers came down and that's why we had to increase the creel numbers and spend a longer time at it. And I think when we finished in '82 we were doing at least six hours a day and finishing a bit earlier in October ... they were getting fished up earlier.

Willie Muir, North Ronaldsay

You could get round them all in about four hours ... it was quite a spell on the oars when you were young [fifteen]. Your hands were sore and your backside. It was very hard on your hands but you turned hard and after a while you didn't bother. *John Cutt, North Ronaldsay*

You just didna throw out your creels at random and expect catches. You had to try things out by trial and error. You never stop learning. *Edwin Groat, Papa Westray*

The rope was about seven fathoms long, inshore fishing size ... I never went more than about five or six fathoms at the most, nowadays they go deeper. I was really an inshore man .... *Jimmy Groat*

We usually tried to go when the sea was out, the tide was out. You had a better chance then to get the creels planted in the ware, where they were kind of hidden. The bait that was used was mackerel. We always brought a barrel of mackerel for bait, salted mackerel. It varied according to the weather but [we got] maybe twenty lobsters occasionally ... it just depended. The second fishing, that was about the month of August, the lobsters were more plentiful then. We put the creels out about the thirteenth of May, depending on the weather and they fished on maybe to the end of June then the lobsters began to get soft in the month of July when they cast their shells. Then we put them out again in maybe the second week of August ... it was just a small dinghy with oars. We'd bring them in in October. The evenings were getting darker then and it wasn't so good for going out. *Jimmy Skea, Sanday*

The first year home I fished with my father ... and creeled which is basically Easter to October fishing ... The only time I got any pay I got a share of the catch but the rest of the year I had to catch rabbits and ship them away to make any pay ... Me father didn't have anything to give us, it was as simple as that ... *Geordie Costie, Westray*

Once July came in they'd get more scarce because that was the time they wouldn't go much about because they were casting their shells. The odd time you could get one, you'd think there were two but it was just a shell ... especially if you didn't get to them regularly ... If you got too many in the creel one would kill the other. *John Cutt*

We never ate the lobsters, maybe a small one. No, that was my money. *Jimmy Groat*

A man called Danny Meil bought all the lobsters, he had a big place in Kirkwall and took all the lobsters. He put them to Billingsgate ... I just gathered enough lobsters to make it worthwhile to get out the boat and took [then] by bus to town ... I had a big box anchored in the sea, near the pier and they might live there for two or three weeks 'til I got enough to take to town ... I tied their claws, you had to. They'd bite you if they could. You get them all in the bottom of the boat and when you'd finished for the day you'd tie their toes ... I got bitten once, I never forgot it. Big lobster got me there. I wasn't watching what I was doing, I was looking at something else and he was looking at me. They know what they are doing. *Jimmy Groat*

We had a lobster kist moored which you put the lobsters in that you caught and we stored them until the end of the week and then we had to go down and put them to the Kettletoft pier when an agent took them … he counted them and shipped them and he got the money and paid us the next week …
Jimmy Skea

Mackerel, or sometimes partans, were used as bait. The mackerel were caught on the way to the creels, salted and stored.

The mackerel were thick then. I remember one evening we had twelve boxes. It didn't take long and salted that down. It was no big deal to catch a box of fish … The best bait they reckon was a comper, a fish that lies on the bottom

with a big head. If you got one of them in your creel you baited the next creel with it and that was usually a lobster the next day.
Anthony Duncan, Burray

It's no easy to catch [mackerel] on the hook, you needed a net … Folk didna eat them then. They thought they wasna fit to eat. Used for baiting the creels, just salted them and kept them in a barrel for going to the creels, but folk eat them now, changed their ideas.
Jimmy Groat

We caught the mackerel with five foot lines. I could see the mackerel rushing in the water and hopefully they would take because sometimes when they are rushing round they don't take, they are looking for the sand eel and you can't catch them, they are after the sand eel. It's only when they are down a bit you can catch them.
Robin Duncan

Gangwarily leaving Kirkwall

Johnnie Flaws, Stromness, 1950s

You would get a big conger eel every now and again about harvest time of the year, about two or three feet long. Monsters. Like a big a snake, it just filled the whole creel, coiled around the creel, they'd bite you if you put your hand near them, we'd open the lid and let them get out. They sometimes get out if they got their head through the net they'd stretch it, slime all over it, a big round hole and he's gone … dirty things … Never ate them, we let them go, put them over the side, get rid of them, glad to see the last of them. They leave a dirty smell in the creel and the lobsters didna like it either, they wouldn't go in.

Jimmy Groat

We had an abundance of partans. Partans were never sold in those days, the only market was for your lobster. We had oodles of partans and fish, that was very much a big part of our living. *Helen Manson*

Partans were sometimes taken ashore and given to people who had no boat, just for eating for themselves. *Jimmy Skea*

Everybody had plenty. You would give your neighbours, old people who didn't have a boat or were too old to go to sea, you gave them but you never sold any of them … you knew who would appreciate a bit of fish or a partan … you didn't give them a live partan, it was cooked and you were sent along with these few partans in a basket. *Helen Manson*

What did you wear to go to the creels?

… long boots and aprons … plastic aprons. Rainy weather you had to wear oilskins and that was it … Sleeve bands to keep your arms dry. *Willie Muir*

Oilskins, but not like the oilskins you have today … we had a coat down nearly to your ankle … you always seemed to be wet across the shoulders … But in that days you had to treat your own oilskins with linseed oil.

Robin Duncan

Just be leather boots. The oilskins were home-made. There was a lady that would sew cotton and it was immersed then in linseed oil, hanged up to dry and that was the oilskin. It would be dried in the summertime, for the winter, and made double. *John Cutt*

Creels were made at home with locally found materials – stone, wood, wire and netting.

It took about a whole day to make a creel. By the time you make the bottom and put the wires on and knit the netting on, that was a whole day's work … You had a big wooden needle and wrapped the rope around and your fingers gauged the size of the mesh … If you made them too big they would crawl out … They would last for years but for the chaps who worked all the year round a lot of them would get smashed with the bad weather … but I was only working during the summer so mine lasted for years. I would stop creeling about harvest time. No time then. That was me finished until next spring.   *Jimmy Groat*

We used to make our own rope. We had a lot of what they call coir rope, big heavy rope up to four inches and they used to unravel that and knit the creels, make the whole thing … Today a lot of them are made out of steel. When I first started everything was made out of wood or cane or boom defence nets as made the bows. They were as strong as could be. We used to tar them. We used to heat the tar and dip them in the tar. It was messy as could be for weeks after but once they got in the sea they dried off.

Anthony Duncan

A hundred creels, all hauled by hand. Two different kinds you got bamboo, you made them wi' bamboo and wood, then you got the wire for the bows. That was a winters' job and you'd get wood for the bottoms and sometimes you'd get the wood off the beach, rip it and make the bottoms and knit the net on them with the eyes. All made by mesel'.

Marcus Hewison, Westray

They were made in the winter evenings … at the tangles all day and the creels in the evening. That's crofting. Hard, long hours. It was supposed to take a full day to make a creel …   *John Cutt*

One of the biggest things that's affected the creel fishing is steel creels. We used to make all our own creels through the winter, wooden creels, same as the other fishermen.

The most you ever got made was three or four hundred … Now wooden creels, being wood, although they are weighed down with cement and stones or whatever, come bad weather they very easily are drove ashore or got knocked to pieces. If you were in strong tide, the tide took them away or raffled them up. Some fishermen didn't make very efficient fishing creels, which was fine in me book because I thought mine was good fishing creels. Now you can buy steel creels off the shelf, shall we say, made to high standard, they fish very well. You'll still lose them in bad weather but weather that you were losing your wooden creels in, your steel ones will be fine … Strong tidal areas which were always good for lobsters, got quite a rest with the strong tides with the wooden creels for you couldna fish it … but with steel creels you fish right through the strong tides so steel creels is the thing that has had the biggest effect on the creel fishing.

Geordie Costie

Willie Thomson (Wullie o'Neven), North Ronaldsay

In the 1960s some fishermen took advantage of grant aid to convert seine netting boats to creel-haulers and went into creel fishing full-time, throughout the year. Technological advances in the shape of hauling gear, mass-produced steel creels and synthetic fibre ropes allowed deeper waters to be worked all year round with the number of creels increasing from thirty or fifty to hundreds, even thousands. These technological changes and the change to full-time creeling have had an impact on the lobster stocks and it is now much more difficult to earn a living from creeling. As early as 1963 calls were being made to re-stock the seabed. When the Flotta Oil Terminal opened in 1972 many creel boat owners went to work at the Terminal but, in the 1970s, a market for previously ignored partans developed and creeling underwent another boom as virgin fishing grounds were explored. Once again, fishing stocks of partans and lobsters are in decline.

I mind when B came home from New Zealand … He was a lobster fisherman and he and his brothers bought a big seine netter, big boat and that was fifty feet and they went round Orkney and cleaned up all the areas with their fifty – a hundred creels and everybody swore for him for they were ruining the fishing grounds for everyone else. They weren't the only ones who were doing it. Nowadays they are working five hundred to a thousand creels. With two men, maybe three men, there are fewer men working more

creels working further afield. Twenty or thirty years ago you could make a good living at the creeling but no now. It's hard graft.   *Mungo Montgomery, Burray*

Gear, as in catching, for creels has improved tremendously. If you are working the old-fashioned creels you will only catch half of what the newer ones will. It doesna help the fishing stocks any.   *Geordie Costie*

Has the amount of lobsters dried up?

They are just not there any longer. Particularly since they started fishing in deep water and in far off land. Some of the local boys are working bush ropes with eighty creels on them, a mile long and they have upward of a thousand creels. They are saying that this time of year, coming up to harvest, they should be getting a lot of lobsters and before they used to get three, four undersized lobsters in each creels but now they are lucky if they are getting one in a bushel. The young lobsters just aren't there and they're no getting the full sized lobsters either.   *Mungo Montgomery*

Were a lot of local boats going out to the creels?

… seven or eight … when I finished it was down to three. I think that one reason for this was the fact that … the number of lobsters were going down a lot and some of the boats weren't very well equipped to fish in deeper waters. And they hadn't had the experience.

Willie Muir, North Ronaldsay

We've very much suffered from under-regulation … it's our only hope. We can make our own decision, we'll no agree about them all. If we don't do this at best we'll have decisions imposed by Edinburgh and at worst we'll have decisions imposed by Brussels and we don't want that.

If you are making a reasonable living out of eight hundred creels then immediately go down to five hundred creels then you are probably not going to make a living and you'll have to go and do something else. We are trying to enhance the stocks for a start off … you can't do it overnight …

Me father used to get very angry at the big boats, fifty feet boats coming up from Kirkwall and Stromness and fishing up the west side of Westray. One or two of them crossed by us one day and he was that mad he nearly had them in the boat … This is why, the North Ronaldsay men, I one hundred per cent understand their predicament. I don't have an answer for it but I have been in exactly the same predicament meself. The only difference is that we joined the ranks of the bigger boats. They speak about losing a few creels to the propellers of the bigger boats and that happens; where the creels run sub-surface with the tide running. When I worked me two or three single lanes the guy came and snagged it. That is one of the hazards of working single lanes with boys working back ropes. The bigger boats have to work further out, ten, twenty miles off shore and they run the hazard of getting their gear towed away by trawlers and that happens. It's just part of the job and you have to try your best to change with changing times.   *Geordie Costie*

I think they would have to put more young ones out right enough. You canna blame the folk for using more creels. They are just trying to make a living. The grants have stopped on the boats and they canna get any assistance to get started up and they go deeply in debt to get going and they have to take more and more risks and go further afield and it's telling on the stuff that's being caught.

Mungo Montgomery

If you are catching you might have nothing but there might be two big lobsters in the next creel, that's what keeps you going … I'm an optimist generally … . there's no point in moaning, nobody pays any attention, just get with it and if it's no working what you're doing then try it different, do something different. If what you are trying at this moment in time is no working well, move ground, change bait or do something different.

By the time I sold the *Enterprise* in 1979 I think we were hauling about four hundred … with the *Bonhomie* we were working with a thousand creels, hauling five hundred each day … [now] I fish from a boat that's nearly a hundred years old. I have a hundred creels and haul fifty a day and I am as happy as I've been for years.

Geordie Costie

Creeling is still popular, full- or part-time, for many Orcadians. Some just keep one creel for a lobster for home, others have taken lobster fishing into the twenty-first century. Robert Smith in St Margaret's Hope comes from a family of creel fishermen and now sells his lobsters all over the world through the Internet.

raham Scott and Ian Deyell creeling, North Ronaldsay

Photo: Helga Tulloch

Mrs Miller and Jessie Chalmers, gutters, Stronsay

HERRING

Herring stations, Papa Stronsay

The herring has a special place in the history of fishing. During the boom years, fortunes were made from the elusive shoals by skippers who followed their annual migrations. To ensure that herring were cured as soon as possible after they had been caught, herring stations were established down the east coast with specially built piers and stores, occupied only for a few months every year. The crews of the drifters stayed on board the boats and had less contact with Orkney people than the gutters who settled locally every year until 1939 when the Second World War ended the industry in Orkney. Herring were still caught until the early 1960s, being landed elsewhere but, by then, fishing stocks had been so depleted that the industry has not been able to revive since.

The heyday of the herring industry, the end of the nineteenth century, has now passed from living memory and there is no one now who worked in the herring industry in Burray or Stromness. There are people, however, who remember the industry in Papa Stronsay and Stronsay. Stronsay was the nearest island to the fishing grounds and had a good harbour, ensuring its survival. Few Orkney boats took part in the whole herring season but some local sail boats joined the fishing fleet for the first part of the season, leaving the steam drifters from Shetland and the east coast to follow the herring down the east coast to Lowestoft in October.

Along with the large number of gutters who came to work in Orkney, there also came foremen, coopers, agents for selling and buying the fish and customs men. This annual influx of people provided a source of income to supplement farming. The economic contribution of the industry is reflected in the Rates bills for Stronsay which were the highest for any parish in Orkney during the 1920s.

It was a great occasion when they came back from the herring fishing because they'd always have so many good things for us. They'd start off by going away to Stornoway. My grandfather would have a crock of butter with him and that would be bartered for a length of Harris tweed. I can remember going to school in Stromness with a suit of Harris tweed.

In a fishing boat there are sixteen shares and you get the profit according to how many shares you've got. If they employ anyone, they are paid hands. Sometimes you'd have two or three people holding shares and one or two paid hands who would get a weekly wage, didn't matter if they fished well or not but very often they would get a bonus if it was a good season.

The herring moved up from Loch Fyne, to Stornoway, Scrabster, to Stromness, to Holm and then to Stronsay. Stronsay was usually the last port of call for her. Some of them went up as far as Scalloway in Shetland but not all of them went, none of them went down to Lowestoft. That was where the herring season finished ... The Stromness market seemed to coincide with the return of the fishermen at the end of the season. *Willie Groat, Longhope*

There was quite a few that went on that herring industry. They went on Stronsay boats ... my father was on a Stronsay boat with his cousin who was lost overboard, the day World War One was declared. He held on to the sail too long and went overboard ... then of course the North Ronaldsay boat used to have a small boat or a pram that they towed with them, but the Stronsay boats didn't have that and, by the time they turned the big boat round, it was too late. He came to the surface once ...

John Cutt, North Ronaldsay

Of course he [my father] cooked on the boat, he was their cook and he made the most attractive dishes, I can still taste them but he left it to the womenfolk when he was at home, he said 'I get plenty of that when I am at sea' and he says 'I'll just leave that to the womenfolk'.

Willie Groat, Longhope

They went out to the fishing at night and they fished through the night. When I came first here, there were sail boats that came here. They went out in the afternoon and they fished all night and they would be going away fifty miles, they went a long distance away and they put out their nets ... I have heard my husband say his father had a herring boat and that was a sail boat ... and, in the summer holidays from the school, he got out with the boat and he remembers being wakened through the night to see the nets coming aboard, all those silver fish pouring into the hold of the boat.

In 1927, when I came here, it was still quite good fishing and quite a number of people were employed ... First, the puffers came with loads of what they called stock, that was barrels and there were yards out there where they worked and cured the herring in the summertime and the barrels were piled on that yard ... ready to be filled when the herring were cured.

My husband was a cooper, he made barrels. There was puffers that came here in the early spring and they brought wood to make the barrels, what the called the staves, and the round end on the top and they made the barrels for that ... Sometimes they got staves that were already bent but often they got staves that needed to be seasoned and curved ...

All herring going to the continent were salted to a different strength. Some countries wanted them lightly salted and some wanted them heavily salted.

For a special cure of herring, in the early season, when the

Gutters, Stronsay

herring were small, the herring were called matties, that was a special light cure of herring and they were cured with Liverpool salt. One year there was a cargo of salt came here to one of the yards in Papay and they lost an awful lot of herring because the salt wasn't up to standard.

The ships came from the continent, Norwegians, Swedes and Germans all came here to buy herring. The buyers came and then the ships came ...   *Meg Fiddler, Stronsay*

Very busy ... and seeing the morning boats, the drifters all coming in ... with their catches. And ... tying up, and it was a squeeze to get into the pier sometimes for a lot of the men ... and the old Harbour Master shouting, and them pushing to get in ... and then they got ashore and took a sample of their herring ... and came up to the Auction Mart ... and they were sold by auction ... in the big room. They tipped out ... their samples and let them see and the curers were around and the lower part of the

place was all divided off into wee offices for the curers and the men looking after the drifters. Then they went away back and the carters got in and carting up the pier, horses and lorries going like anything.   *James Work, Stronsay*

They were sold every morning, where the fish market is now. They started at eight o'clock in the morning. Two men from the drifter came up with a sample of fish, a sample of herring in a herring basket and that was put out on a metal tray and the buyers came and if they thought it was good herring they were sold by auction.

There was a time came when the drifters were only allowed to catch a certain amount of herring and it caused an awful lot of ill feeling because the ones that came in the morning sold their fish and when so many had been sold then the remainder were sold at a very cut price and the people that came in late felt they were dealt with ill. They hoisted a red flag. That was the sign that there was no more herring going into the sale ring and the rest would be sold just at a block price.   *Meg Fiddler, Stronsay*

You see there were a lot of people living round the village then. Then all that bigger houses up through the village ... they are standing yet, those houses are more or less just as they were. But they were big houses for that times and they had extended their houses ... the curers would take up their wives and families with them ... and they nearly all had lodgers during the summertime ... making quite a bit of money off of that.

Any place that had the opportunity ... and a great number of them did. It's the same as what I told you, like my mother was selling cheese and butter and whatever she could make, and then the ... tatties and a great lot of the cattle were taken down in the summertime, all gaining a bit, well, it was an outlet for the produce. It was all the beef they went for. They were getting a bit extra besides shipping them away. The main thing on the small crofts was the men getting the job over the summertime, and work down there.

The crofters and farmers during the wintertime had no connection with it, they were off, the carting jobs were all finished when the last of the herring was shipped, shipped to the continent ... quite big boats came in too. There was no coal to fill but they were back working on the farms again that was off until the first boat appeared in the summertime, usually about the first of June, stock boats would start to cart up salt and supplies. Filling salt they said was a very hard job, the boys used to complain about that. The coal business went on constantly for there were coasters running coal ... all the time to keep it supplied. That coal merchants made a good thing. They would have made money there's no question about that.

James Work, Stronsay

Photo: Orkney Library, Photographic Archive

...sh workers, Stronsay, with a salt store and living quarters in the background.

The gut boats carried the guts from Papa Stronsay to Stronsay for the gut factory. There was nothing lost … all that guts was collected in barrels and the gut factory put it into fishmeal.   *Robbie Sutherland, Stromness*

They were old ships anchored off Stronsay and the coal boats came up from south and dumped it into the coal hulks and, usually on a Monday when the fleet were going out to their first session of the week, they would go along the hulks and re-coal. It was mostly coal boats in those days … the coal hulks were permanently staffed … it was mostly Westray men and they kept the fleets supplied with coal …   *Jack Scott, Papa Stronsay*

There was four hulks there. There was one belonging to Chalmers of Stronsay, called the *Hebe* there was another belonging to Duncan and Jameson which was an old steel sail ship. Our ship was the *Watchful,* which was a coaster. They took her up here, took the engines out of her, towed her to Stronsay. She was moored in Stronsay … There was another one, which was concrete. They made concrete barges during the First World War and two of them lay here and the one was converted into a hulk and towed to Stronsay.

We had small coasters that came up [from the Tyne], we usually had one a week and when the drifters landed their herring they would come along and bunker, that's coal … They had to bunker every second or third day. There was just wee holes along the side, coal scuttles and we had four hundredweight tubs of coal, and that was lifted up [by the ship's derrick] out of the hold and tipped into their bunker … we usually had two men from Westray and two men from Burray … They lived in the fo'c'sle of the ship and we had a skipper that lived in midships and an engineer

Landing the herring catch, Stronsay

... She was ballasted with coal for the winter. She was very perfectly moored. The big anchors came from Lyness, you know, salvaged. We had two anchors and a swivel and then two chains up to the bows of the ship and she would just swing around ...   *Robbie Sutherland, Stromness*

It looked beautiful. They were far bonnier boats ... a whole line of that steaming out. It was a great sight. And another thing, they were two or three bakehouses going in the island ... There was a son of one of the bakers, where the bakehouse is standing, the house standing end-on to the street, below the middle of the village ... His father was the head baker in there ... and when he was a boy he said he was turfed out and he had to go up to a skylight window at the upper end of the bakehouse, and he had to count the number of boats that was appearing round on this point for Stronsay. By nine o'clock in the morning, if there were a certain number of boats appeared, there was another batch of bread to go in. That's how they gauged it.

James Work, Stronsay

The fishermen had to take care of their nets as they decayed rapidly. They had to be treated and were laid out in fields, leased locally, to dry.

They used to spread them out on the ... Ness [behind the east side of the village]. That was a job that anybody with a cart would do, cart up nets for them. They'd get them back on Monday morning. I mind it being odd seeing the back of that Ness black ... I mind the men working there on a Saturday afternoon turning out and working the nets.

James Work, Stronsay

We got all sorts of continental wines and spirits, cherry brandy and peppermint wine ... but you had to be very careful because there was always two customs men here, just for the fishing, just while the herring were being shipped out in the big ships.   *Meg Fiddler, Stronsay*

Curing the herring with salt was the only way that the fish could be preserved for export journeys to Europe. The gutters were generally seen to be a very happy group of women. Although their wages were low and their working conditions harsh, they had a lifestyle which was unusually independent and social for women at the time.

There was twenty of us in the isle [Papa Stronsay] and suddenly one beautiful day in summer three hundred girls appeared ... it was quite a business. They took them in by special boat. We used to go down, past the huts to school and when these girls appeared we used to go the back road. There was such a lot of them ... they were Gaelic speakers and we didn't know what the dickens they were saying to us you see ... some of them used to chase after us and we were just boys at the time. In fact one day I was down with my brother at the pier and some of the girls caught him and put in the hut and I had to go home for help to get him out. Oh, they weren't doing him any harm, it was just the fun of it, I suppose.

Jack Scott, Papa Stronsay

The women and the men were accommodated in wooden huts ... when the herring was landed it was taken up manually and then they were in like wooden tubs and the herring were put in and the girls just worked that. The girls worked three girls to a crew and they had one cooper who was above them. He attended to the barrels that they were putting the herring into and at the same time he had to examine those barrels to see that they had packed them properly because some women were very careless ... They cut the herring up to the throat but some of them were careless and they didn't take all the inside out and that wouldn't cure ... they worked long, long hours in the summertime ... if there was a big fishing they would be working until maybe one or two o'clock and they always wanted to get the herring in the barrels as fresh as possible and then they started again at six o'clock in the morning.

The girls all stayed in huts, there would be six in a hut ... their mothers had done it before them and they really were a happy crowd. Sometimes there would be a father, a mother and children would come and they would come to the school for two or three weeks in the summertime. The father would be a cooper, the mother would be a gutter and the children would have to come with them.

I was a in a gutters' hut, they had bunk beds and a little stove with a pipe coming up through the roof. They didn't have much room but they were really very happy.

If they didn't have a big catch then they would have the evening off, it was a very hard life and they didn't have many comforts.

They had Monday off and they would go about, very clean and tidy and they would go about knitting. Knitting, knitting, knitting and all the fishermen all had a blue pullover, a gansey, they knitted that for the fishermen, they were great knitters. There were two rest huts with facilities for games, they could go there if their fingers got bad. Their fingers got cut and the salt seemed to eat into the cut. There were two nurses, one from the Church of England and one from the Church of Scotland and they would dress those fingers for them in the rest huts. They often had parties and dances in the huts at the weekend … they could go to it if they weren't working on the herring. They always seemed to be holding parties in their huts at the weekend and the boys used to go there then … there were one or two girls who married here.

The boats didn't go out until after twelve o'clock on a Sunday night and some of them didna go out until the Monday and so there was no herring on a Monday and that would be a day when the girls would be filling up the barrels in the yards … sometimes they would come in with a big catch and sometimes a very light catch. The men about the pier would say they all knew the drifters and their names and they would say 'Here comes so and so and they seem to have a good catch' because they would see them deep in the water.

Meg Fiddler, Stronsay

The herring was taken off the drifters in baskets and they had a trolley on rails that came down the station on rails and Sinclair Buchan had a motor vehicle to drive them up but most of the other stations just had a trolley and pushed them up by hand.

There was one gutter who could do sixty a minute … She was an expert. My dad counted her, he was watching her … and he counted the herring, sixty a minute.

Jack Scott, Papa Stronsay

They wore rubber boots and oilskin skirts and ordinary women's clothes … They had an oilskin apron with a bib on it, and straps on it and it depended on the weather they might have a cotton top. Usually over their heads they had a kind of square that they took over their heads and they seemed to cross it here and tie it at the back of their heads. They had bandages on their hands to save their fingers, for they were sharp knives and if they cut their hands the salt stopped it from healing, seemed to eat into their hands.

Meg Fiddler, Stronsay

They wore … black oilskin … aprons … high up around them, tied around them and a cloth on their head. Most of their fingers [were] all wrapped up, with a cloth, a bandage around their fingers for cutting with the sharp knife, you see, and they were ripping at such a speed.

James Work, Stronsay

They had to work outside in all weathers … They liked a day like this with a ruffle in the sea because that made the herring move and come up and they were using floating nets then.

That East Coast fishermen were tremendous singers. And their dress was a blue suit and a blue jersey, that was their dress. Like a Sunday night service they came into that all dressed the same. Sankey hymns. The Kirk was catering for

it … they had a station. Two women came down and ran a sort of rest home, rest hut they called it, for them … The girls went in there a great lot, for recreation … and they bandaged up cut fingers and all this sort of thing for them.

They sang and they were beautiful singers, on a Sunday night there were Sunday evenings in the little church that was down here and even the local people went there, just to hear them singing the redemptions, the redemption hymns, that's all that they would sing.

Meg Fiddler, Stronsay

Through the week they were working … in the evenings the lasses would have been gutting herring still if there was a big rush of herring on late … They were busy all the time. Saturday they would have been dressed and out. I never heard any disturbance. There were two policemen put out here for the summer. There was no question of locking doors or any such thing as that. They were really very good people.

James Work, Stronsay

The barrel boat arriving with the season's barrels

In the summertime sometimes our boat would be pinched by the drifters' men coming across from Stronsay to see the girls in Papay and they would be desperate to get back to their boats on the Monday and they would pinch our boat … My dad didn't worry but they never tied it up and it would drift and so what they did then was they put all the boats off to a buoy in the bay and had a wee dinghy which they came ashore and locked it in an outhouse.

Some of the men took a great farling, you know what they gutted the herring in and took it and went over the sea in hid. One fella swam across, it wasn't very far … he tied his clothes on his head and away he went.

One summer my father decided he would do a night service [between Papa Stronsay and Stronsay] and it nearly finished him. He got as poor and thin as could be from lack of sleep so he only did that one year.   *Jack Scott, Papa Stronsay*

At that time you did not dance on Sunday morning and through the week, there was little, oh, maybe among the

huts they would have had an accordion going and a bit of local thing but they were that busy they were no just organised like in the hall or anything, I never mind that … well Saturday afternoon they were drying nets and cleaning nets and then … coiling up, then on Monday morning they were steaming for the fishing grounds again as fast as they could. It was a right sight to see that boats going out the harbour and around Papa Stronsay.   *Jim Work, Stronsay*

It felt as flat as a flounder when they went. It did feel very flat when they went 'til you got used to it again.

They had a foy, a big do, and all the people gathered at the end of the season.   *Jack Scott, Papa Westray*

One of the main reasons we got rid of her [the coal hulk, the *Watchful*] was debt. The fishermen couldn't pay for their bread, they couldn't pay for their coal. It was pretty hard in 1937.   *Robbie Sutherland, Stromness*

The huts were taken away in 1939 to put up for the thousands and thousand of troops there were in Orkney.

Meg Fiddler, Stronsay

The last summer was '39 and then in September the war started but, even before the war started, they were starting getting employment huts and aerodromes and the surplus labour on the island was taken up with that …

A lot of it was going to Germany … when the war started there was being a lot of herring shipped that summer, it started in August, in September the curers hadn't been paid and of course they couldn't get the money out and they were really quite hard up. I don't know if they ever sorted it out after the war but that certainly happened. A big boat's load of herring was worth quite a lot of money.

James Work, Stronsay

Willie Craigie and Sandy Donaldson, Rousay

INSHORE FISHING

Fishing from the waters close into the land has been part of the Orcadian way of life since people first lived in Orkney. Many households near the shore would have a boat of some sort, a dinghy or a yole which they used to fish the inshore waters.

Cuithes* were plentiful and could reliably be found in safer inshore waters, unlike the elusive herring. Fishing for cuithes or sillocks was an important contribution to the diet but it was also an enjoyable pastime. Mostly the fishing was done in the summer months in the long evenings. Often children went with parents or older siblings, boys and girls together.

Some of the crofters, when weather permitted and they had time to spare, they used to go to the cuithes … in the summer evenings … at the back end o' the year if it was a fine day they would go fishing … the days were short and it would be nearly dark when they got ashore with the fish … When they got the boat hauled up and secured, there was usually a number of folk there to meet them and the fish would be parted, shared out into different lots … They had oil lanterns, you see … sometimes some of the smaller fish would be cooked that night. They were very sweet, the little sillocks … they used to curl up in the frying pan. They are best the night they are caught.

Jenny Tulloch, North Ronaldsay

During harvest you would get the sillocks … it was always in the evening … maybe stop working with the horses about four o'clock and go off then, depends on the time of year … I liked the fun for one thing, the excitement of catching the cuithes, especially when they were plentiful … I seen the sillocks, catching them by the hundred … I've seen two on the one hook sometimes …

Jimmy Groat, Copinsay

It was more for a pastime, they did it in the fine weather in the summertime. It didna need to be a big catch of fish to do the island. There was always people going out to the cuithes … *Meg Fiddler, Stronsay*

Unless they were really well cleaned they widna keep. The fish had to be cleaned very thoroughly, where the guts had been you put a small amount of salt, then lay them in a wooden barrel in a criss-cross and you would leave them in there for three days … which meant they werenae too salty. They were taken out, you gave them a wash before you started drying them. And you spread them out on dykes and walls … If it was a good dry day you spread the fish out, if it came rain you nipped out and took the fish in and you finished them off inside. You would hang them up inside on the pulley … and then you would wrap them in newspaper and store them in a dry outhouse.

Some people tied them in pairs and hung them over the line but nowadays the gulls are so ferocious, last time I heard someone hung them on a line he had no sooner hung them out than they had disappeared. Before he had turned his back they were down and nipped the fish away, that was just two or three years ago. *Harcus Scott, Westray*

It wasn' uncommon to catch a bucketful. I remember once we caught a bathful, at least two buckets, there were hundreds. It took a while to gut them. It was worse than skinning rabbits … We left the heads on, that was how we hung them on the line. You don't want them every day but they were quite good to eat … They would keep for long enough, they would keep them a year.

Jimmy Groat, Copinsay

*Coalfish are known in Orkney by a number of different names. Until its first year the fish is called a sillock, then in its second year a piltock. Most frequently heard is cuithes which is the coalfish from its first to third year. After the third year they are known as laithe or greyfish. The fully grown greyfish is known as a saithe.

Collecting bait

Fish drying, Rousay

Photo: Orkney Library, Photographic Archive

It might be three in a boat or so, just prams, they used to buy the flies from the shop for the cuithes. Sometimes they made them and then they tied the feathers to hooks with catgut.

They salted them and dried them … they used to hang them on the fire indeed, near the grate, a lot of folk had open grates then, they had stoves and ranges … You pulled the skin off when they got hard. They dried them outside in the sun first of course, then they took them inside, near the grate … at the back end of the year there wasn't so much sun for drying fish so they were salted, then they were taken out of the salt, they were what they called dry salted. They were so long in the pickle then they were dried and it was good. They were usually split open. Half the bone was taken out before they were dried.

Jenny Tulloch, North Ronaldsay

Whitefish were caught with a hand line or a rod, baited with limpets or occasionally mussels. At one time there had been an export of dried cod but this had ceased by 1914. The fish caught were usually for use by the family and friends rather than for sale like the lobsters, but, if it was possible to get to a market such as Kirkwall, then they could also be sold. Commercial line fishing was overtaken when trawling became more common from the end of the nineteenth century. Trawling was blamed for the decline in numbers of cod and haddock for line fishermen. Fishing for cod and haddock or plaice was a rather more serious occupation than fishing for cuithes as the water where you would find the bigger whitefish was further out into the tides and usually it was the occupation of men. The whitefish were very much valued for their size and flavour. Fish was eaten fresh, salted or dried.

He'd go to the shore the day before and gather limpets and dee them, just put them in the water long enough for them to come out of their shells easily then they were all baited up.
Helen Manson, South Ronaldsay

I fished all the summertime, hauled haddocks, and caught rabbits all the winter. That's what we did for a living. So it was lobsters and there was not velvets then of course, just lobsters and then you got the haddocks then in the summertime …
Marcus Hewison, Westray

When there was big cod fishing on, they went about three miles out into the Firth and set their lines, they had baskets and baskets, huge, beautiful white fleshed cod, sometimes they got halibut and skate, big skate.
Helen Manson, South Ronaldsay

Every summertime you'd get plenty, go up there and maybe get as many as twenty score in a day if it were a good day and you're working right …. It was the first of the flood, it depends, when they are out and you'd work them for so long … I'd get up in the morning and haul me creels and then haul haddocks and sometimes I'd some haul again on the way back when I was close in … in those days you could haul twice in a day and get a lobster both times …. [for the haddock] we'd use sprolls, just a loop of wire, like a half moon with a bit of lead in the middle o'it and each end then had a bit of string with a swivel on it and a hook on it at each end. Then of course the lead in the middle as a weight to sink it and then you'd tie long line to that … you'd use lugworms, dig them out of the sands or limpets but worms was the best … I chopped them on a stone and put bits o'them on … I never chewed them, I don't fancy the taste of them.

Marcus Hewison, Westray

We caught cod with a hand line and used limpets for bait. Latterly it was just flies we worked with … The cod was just going out on the tide into the Firth. We didna sell any, we never got that many to sell, we didna get enough. I mind one year we got a good run o' cod, we got a good haul but we salted most of them. *Angus Heddle, Longhope*

We were taken down the Pentland Firth to fish for cod … It was frightening in many ways. We fished on the ebb tide. There's a waterfall off Brims … and that is where you caught the cod because everything was falling over the edge there. The cod were there to feed. We'd set our lines to the depth, we had limpet baits on the hooks. You didn't haul away on the line, oh no, you watched the swell and, as the swell went down, you pulled on the line very smartly and as the boat went up again there was a small cleat there and you made fast, so it automatically pulled the fish up again, and in the next wave going down you did it again. They were big cod and my grandfather had a harpoon and when he saw the mouth of the fish come up he plunged the harpoon down their throat so that, if the fish did get off the hook, it couldn't possibly turn and swim downwards, and put a noose on it's tail and haul it on board. Dogfish were dangerous, even if you thought they were dead they still could snap at you and made a nasty mark on your leg.

Halibut were also fished there and of course, if you got a big halibut, maybe a hundredweight and a half and they were worth a lot of money, so we didn't go straight home that day, we'd signal to the lighthouse at Cantick. (The Assistant Keepers at Cantick were my grandfather's first cousins and he would signal to them … and we would sail on and they would come down and tell my granny, who was their auntie that the boat had gone straight on …) and we'd go into Scapa. Now my brother John and I would be detailed to run into Kirkwall and go to Scott's fish shop and

we had a note of the size of the fish and the weight of the fish. We'd go in there and tell them that we were landed at Scapa pier. We were given, maybe, half a crown each and told to be back in fifteen minutes and we'd raid the shops in that time … this was our benefit and we'd raid the shops and get all the good things. We knew where to go, exactly. Then we got back with the van which would go out and get the halibut, sometimes cod as well and the cash was paid over for weight of the fish and we'd sail back then.

Willie Groat, Longhope

You dig lugworm and go out to the North Sound or go up the lighthouse area and fish for haddocks with a thing called a sproll. There were two hooks on it, held apart by a piece of strong wire. It was a great thrill catching haddock, the first time you hauled up your line and pulled up a couple of haddocks. *Harcus Scott, Westray*

When my grandfather got a nice six-pounder cod and he'd open it up and pull out the liver. It was greasy and he'd put it between two pieces of bannock and eat it and the cod liver would be running down his beard and we weren't allowed to be sick. If you were sick you were never allowed to go again.

The end of January into the month of February was when the cod roe were in season and that was a particularly good time to fish for cod. Then the fish would be cleaned and dried and put out to dry. Dried cod would be in season in the springtime. You wouldn't get cod in the May/June because bluebottle would be out then and they would infest the fish … but because it was salted and hard, the bluebottle had no effect. Salted it first in brine. The recipe for the saltness was a potato, if the potato just floated below the surface then that was the right mixture of salt to the water …

When we came home from the fishing we would clean the fish at the shore and if there were otters about we'd throw the waste to them and they'd come running to us.

Willie Groat, Longhope

The north west shore was by far the best. You got haddock and ling as well as mackerel. One day we got six barrels in one day. That was full load.

The problem wi' cod was it was more a winter fish. It was hardly ever weather to go out. You just have to go a bit off the land to get some … *Willie Muir, North Ronaldsay*

It supplemented the diet. It was a fine healthy food the fish, at one time they used to eat the livers [mixed with oatmeal] … they must have been chock full of vitamins.

Jenny Tulloch, North Ronaldsay

Fishing yole

Angus Brown fishing with a handline, Hoy

Usually came ashore then geid a half share to the boat and then the other ones, half between us. If there's somebody with me then we'd put them in three shares and when you came to the beach, you parted them out in three shares, evenly, then one of you turned your back roond and somebody pointed to the fish and said 'Whaur owns those ones?' That's what decided who got what, because you'd sometimes get bigger ones in the bunches then there is no cheating then.

We always had fresh ones to ourselves and salted ones for the winter then divided them on top of the roof then took them in and hung them up for wintertime.

Marcus Hewison, Westray

There wasnae much cod to be had … the trouble was that the cod got scarce here. The trawlers ruined the cod fishing long afore the war you know. The cod fishing depleted greatly and they blamed the trawlers for cleaning the grounds.

My grandfather long, long ago made a lot of money out of the cod fishing but it was never the same after the trawlers cleaned the grounds, they broke up the fish beds and destroyed things.

It was a very independent class of people long ago compared to now. It didn't matter if it snowed or blowed they had plenty of milk, plenty o' meal, plenty o' tatties, plenty o' herring and dried cod. Didn't need to worry.

Willie Mowatt, South Ronaldsay

Gutting the catch

Gutting fish

Fish have been an important part of the Orcadian diet since people first came to live in Orkney. If you could not catch your own fresh fish then you had either to eat salted fish or buy from passing boats.

The merchants sold salt fish. They were hard, dried, huge fish, ling or cod and they were as hard as bricks and it was a job to cut them. *Jenny Tulloch*

We could go and help ourselves to herring at any of the stations so we had herring quite a lot .... my mother used to make potted herring and I liked hid but after a lot of days eating herring on and off it tends to put you off. *Jack Scott*

You scaled them, you got them and they were crumpled up type things and you cleaned them and took the roes out of them, the soft roes and the hard roes and you boiled them, for about maybe twenty minutes to half an hour and if you didna like them very salt you put them in cold water and took them to the boil and you poured that water off and repeated the process and that took some of the salt out o' them ... Children didn't usually like salt herring. 'Too many bones in them' they used to say ...

I loved salt herring, even in later years in the last ten years I often had salt herring, you can get them now in Kirkwall.

... and the herring and the tatties were boiled in the same pot because the tatties took some of the salt out of the salt herring but I used to boil them separate. *Jenny Tulloch*

The cod roe, that was beautiful, a real delicacy

Helen Manson

Every house in Stronsay had at least a half barrel of salt herring. It was a taste that you had to acquire. Now salt herring is quite a delicacy but then ... it was for the poorer people. If you acquired a taste for them they were really wonderful. *Meg Fiddler*

We had the idea that they [mackerel] were not very good to eat. That's what the old folk said, so we never tried them. but in the end we did and found that they were very tasty. You had to cook them very early. Once or twice we had them when we came back from the fishing and they were delicious, I must say. *Willie Muir*

When I went to school there was no school lunches, we just took a piece with us. When you got home your dinner was usually heated up what the folk'd had at dinnertime and heated up salt fish left a bit to be desired, I can assure you. We had a cat at that time that was particularly interested and he would get a bite and I would get a bite. I used to feed the cat copious quantities of salt fish.

Harcus Scott

I remember someone from Sanday coming to sell fish at the pier. Herring for a half a crown a dozen *Jenny Tulloch*

We were quite used to whitefish because we lived near the pier and if there was a trawler came in then my father would go down and give them a hand to moor up if the Harbour Master wasn't available. It was a great thing to be down there first and get the ropes because you would always get fish. We used to get ling and skate and tusk and things that werna so common. *Harcus Scott*

I can mind in the general merchants business when the van gied oot and there would have be a fair sized bucket filled with salt herring ... When I was in the shop, in 1962, I used to sell two and and half barrels of salt herring a year. That was about the cheapest diet you could have ... it would have been good for you I suppose.

We got a lot of fish, but that was purely because my father was Pier Master and he was aye given a lot of fish off the boats that came in. *Edwin Groat/John P Drever, Westray*

Bill Laughton selling fish in Stromness

FULL-TIME FISHING

In the early part of the twentieth century there were only a few full-time fishermen. There were five Burray zulus fishing with the herring fleets but other than that, only small yoles worked the local waters, catching fish to sell locally. There were no Orkney-owned bigger boats catching fish to sell to markets south until after the Second World War.

Stromness was more of a Merchant Service town, however, there were probably sixteen full-time fishermen. In Stromness the slipways that you see had a yole laid up during the winter months. This period was used to refit or repair the yoles and make fishing gear. Generally the boats were owned by two fishermen, who crewed the boats. The days of sail had passed and the boats were motorised, however most boats carried mast, sails and oars for emergencies as total faith in the motor took some time to develop. Some of the fishermen had a spare, smaller boat, square sterned. They fished for haddock, mackerel and ling for the local market. Also for crabs and lobsters. I remember when huge shoals of sillocks came in around our piers and these were caught by circular nets. In fact the shoals were so thick one could not see the seabed.

Robbie Sutherland, Stromness

Alfie Sinclair was so determined to work at the fishing that he packed up his job with a building firm, leaving his father no choice but to take him away to the fishing.

We were always involved with the fishing. My father had a small boat. The only way I could get into this boat was to pack my job up and … I started off working lines, small lines, you know … when weather was permitting. We would go out and get the bait, roughly about five hundred hooks on each line. He actually sold fish with a barrow and went way up the street.

At that time a big boat was about twenty-two feet long, that was a big boat in Orkney at that time … He used to take

Seine netters at Stromness Pier in the 1950s. James Harvey, the Harbour Master, is sitting on the bollard

fish home in the winter when the weather was bad [on one of the North of Scotland boats] from Aberdeen or Shetland and he went round and sold fish and so on.

It was actually a Shetland skiff, it was a good working boat at that time … catching mainly haddock, we used to go to the creels for perhaps a month in the year … We used to land our fish, we got eight shillings a hundredweight … we just took the petrol and expenses off and the rest was just divided two or three ways according to the number of crew.

It was all engines that came out of cars, old Morris engines … they were no longer fit to run a car but we kept them going in them boats … There was a few Kelvin engines but the Kelvin engines used to break down far more than the old car engines … We never carried sails but we did carry big oars … If any boat got into any kind of bother, you were always watching just in case.

We would leave four o'clock in the morning, maybe in the summertime maybe half past two or three in the morning and then back in about eleven o'clock and then you had to go and sell all this, then you had to bait your lines for the next day so it meant that you did most of your work ashore.

We used mainly mussels or dig lugworm at the north end of the harbour here. It was mainly mussels. We used to go round to Waulkmill Bay there with the boat and we could take maybe a ton and a half of mussels … and we would get on board and just wait until the tide floated us and that kept us going for some time. *Alfie Sinclair, Stromness*

Although Orkney did not have its own trawler fleet in the early twentieth century, steam trawlers from Hull, Grimsby and Aberdeen visited Orkney on their way to the fishing grounds. It was exhausting work and Orkney shores have seen many trawlers lost on the way to and from the fishing grounds.

Stromness at that time had a big fishing visitation … the Grimsby trawlers going away to Iceland and that sort of way. They used to load up in Grimsby and come by Stromness and load up their coals to take them there and back when they did the same. As a boy I had a chum that

The *Enterprise* of Wick

came up from Grimsby. His father was Captain of one of the trawlers … It was his holidays so his father used to know he was coming in past here and going fishing for a fortnight and he would pick him up on the way back so he was friends with [local people].

The Aberdeen trawlers were weekly boats but the Grimsby and Hull were fortnightly … a lot of them were called after football teams, the *Leicester City* and so forth. In fact the *Leicester City* went on the rocks on the face of Hoy, we watched it just breaking up, it was a bad winter and there was nothing there within months. The last thing that was there was the boiler. We had eight of the their coffins on the *Ola* at one time … A lot of them, they set their course and they didn't allow for the flood coming in Hoy Sound and it took a bad drag on them. Hoy has accounted for an awful lot of trawlers … They were literally on deck for twenty-four hours a day while they were fishing, while the fish were there, gutting and cleaning so they were exhausted by the time they were going home. They very often tied the wheel and set the course so there maybe would have been nobody on watch …

Walter Leask, Stromness

We used to listen to the trawlers talking. They would speak to home sometimes. You'd hear them going to come and lie in the bay here in bad weather and you used to go down then and get a fry of fish … I've seen a lot of trawlers in here when the weather was poor. Some of them come in the shore up the pier, that was when you got the baskets of fish from them … they were catching all kinds of things, cod and haddock and flatfish and stuff, just the very best.

Angus Heddle, Longhope

In the wintertime a number of trawlers called, mainly for shelter during bad weather. Occasionally they required coal (bunkers). The trawlers and trawlermen were a great source of entertainment for the youngsters. Although Stromness was 'dry', no drink sold either in the hotels or shops, the ocean going trawler carried bond ie cigarettes, sweets and liquor. The young lads would sometimes get sweets and tobacco and some would get duff. They would also go for messages or advise the call girls.

Robbie Sutherland, Stromness

The history of fishing in Orkney is, with the exception of fishing for cuithes or inshore creeling, not one of continuous tradition. It is one of change, adaptation and experiment.

It wasn't until the 1950s that Orcadians moved to full-time, all year round fishing. It has been said that land in Orkney is so fertile that people have neglected the commercial opportunities of the sea.

Boats worked away for periods of up to two weeks and, depending on the crewing arrangement, the crews would get home for between four and ten days. In 1969 the Reid brothers paid £56,000 for 'The Bountiful', a trawler/seine netter which, at seventy-two feet, was the largest vessel in the Orcadian fleet.

At the same time Angus Sinclair had the 'Responsive', the largest whitefishing boat in Orkney. Although the Orcadian fishing fleet cannot rival the Shetland fleet for fishing power or numbers, entrepreneurs like the Reid brothers, the Costies, Malcolm Brown and the Bain brothers re-invented the whitefishing industry in Orkney. Orkney Fishermen's Association was started to represent fishermen's interests in times of increasing regulation and legislation.

Where possible, boats worked from Orkney, landing their catches in Kirkwall, Stromness, Westray, Wick, Scrabster, Thurso, the West Coast or Aberdeen. The introduction of ice plants in Stromness and Kirkwall, together with fish processing plants, meant that it was possible to land catches in Orkney and so easier to work from home. The availability of fish stocks meant that latterly the boats have had to work a long way from home. If the fishing grounds are far from Orkney, the boats are sometimes left in the nearest port and the crew fly home for their time off.

Alfie Sinclair's father was a full-time small line fisherman. Alfie had the first purpose built seine netter in Orkney (the 'Evelyn') and his sons, Angus and Ollie Sinclair own the 'Orcades Viking III', the largest vessel in Orkney with a crew of over forty.

The *Evelyn*

Photo: courtesy Evellyn Gunn

I thought I could see a future in it. This small boats was so limited so I started working on boats which had four or five of a crew and we could live on board and carried ice so we could go for a few days at a time.

I was working with my uncle who had a vast experience, who was one of the top skippers at the time ... I worked with him for a number of year and then set up myself.

There was no seine netters working out of Orkney at that time, then I got a seine netter ... There was an awful lot of teething troubles because I didn't know enough about it ...

Stromness was really busy at that time. There were nearly thirty or forty Lossiemouth and Buckie boats here every night in the wintertime ... they were all seine net boats. There was a big fleet that used to come out of Wick and Thurso.

It took us some time to get to where we could work the net and where we couldn't ... the seine net could only work on sand. I spent a lot of time round Cape Wrath and then I came back here. I think some of the experience out at the lines certainly helped me out here.

Alfie Sinclair, Stromness

For anybody that's willing to work hard and save their money it's as good a job as I know of. You can become a millionaire at that job easier than any other job that I know of. *Alex Costie, Westray*

If you worked hard you made a living and if lady luck is with you, you made a bigger one. If she turned her back on you, you were in trouble. *John Davisdson, Shapinsay*

Johnny, my brother-in-law, used to go fishing with Norman, my husband, and they were normally either dredging for scallops or creeling but at times they would go to the nets for the haddock, then they would take on a teenage boy for the duration and there just seemed not to be one available,

so I went instead. I was quite excited at the prospect of going to the whitefishing, you know, there might be some money in it but there wasn't at all. In fact I got paid less than I would have got working at the tables in the factory. I found it boring and frightening by turns ... My mother had gone to sea to be a cook on a dredger when I was in my teens ... so she already had no regard for allegedly girls' jobs or boys' jobs. *Julie Gibson, Rousay*

The first trip, if it wasnae for the fact that we landed in Aberdeen I wouldna have gone back. After the second trip I was alright ... just feeling sick and you'd think it was stone mad, it seemed like it wasn't safe but once you got used to it, it was alright. *Anon*

It was hairy once ... we were waiting out to the west for the weather to get better in great big swells, great big ocean swells. Norman and Johnny were quite happily sitting at the back occupying themselves fishing for haddock with long lines instead of the net and I just felt sick. The only time I felt sick. Just watching the sounder so you could actually mark the waves going up, going up then plateauing, then down the other side. It sort of charted waves of nausea.
Julie Gibson, Rousay

Prior to modern navigational aids, fishermen could identify pieces of water with particular names, many of which are still in use.

We had that many names. Names you would never think about ... just out here we had Stormy Bank, and then we had the Sule, then we had the Stack, then a peedie bit off the Brough of Birsay we used to call it 'Bob', Brough of Birsay, you see ... *Alfie Sinclair, Stromness*

Fishermen were not entirely at liberty to choose where they could fish. The three-mile limit was introduced to protect fishing stocks and the living of inshore fishermen. Not everyone took notice of these regulations.

I can assure you it is most embarrassing if you are caught with your gear down in these positions ... the fishery cruisers ... I've been picked up three or four times ... I've been in and charged three or four times ... They had a job to do. It was just a calculated risk.

If the cruiser was coming down then word came down to say that he was coming. They'd ask you where you were and they'd say 'Better get on your bike'.

Alfie Sinclair, Stromness

Living conditions on board were sometimes difficult but living and working so closely often made crew members close.

You just work as a team, like a family. I'll tell you one thing, anything that was said on board or took place on board was never carried ashore. It was like a family. Any wee bits of problem was just kept among the crew ... it is different now, when I started one thing you never discussed was your wages. It didn't matter what happened, you never discussed your wages ...

Usually we had someone who was down as cook but if we didn't have a cook on board then usually it was the first one that got hungry.

We used to eat fish about two or three times a week. It was nothing but the best that we kept for ourselves..

Alfie Sinclair, Stromness

There were never many people who wanted to be cook but someone got elected to cook. A lot of boats just worked turn about, at cooking. If there was any Wickers on board they always seemed to be the cooks for some reason, I don't know why.

Anon

It was a really pretty boat, it was a little old Banffy barrel, everything was wood and brass ... I thought it was cute ... there were four bunks and they were less cute because they had had people in them in ... fishy clothes in sleeping bags on these mattresses for many moons and they were like ... coffins with a long window on one side ... and it was all very damp ... but the engines kept this room warm. So it was warm and damp and smelly. Of course if it was rough, you got your bits banged on the top, the bottom and the sides of these bunks. It did hinder falling out, which was what was intended.

Julie Gibson, Rousay

A seine netter from Lossiemouth. Fish was gutted as soon as possible, boxed, then taken to market for the following day.

It had a loo in the engine room which meant that the loo actually got rather warm, almost to the point of hot … you had to be very careful when you flushed, to open the sea cock before you flushed … You couldn't stand upright, you had to crouch your way to get round the engine. It was alright though. Better than having to go over the side.

Julie Gibson, Rousay

We came into a spell of poor brood years for fish. Haddock were scarce in this waters. There were a lot of small haddocks but no much big stuff. I went scalloping for a few years down the west coast … we were doing long trips, we were doing three weekends away and home for a long weekend … There was other Orkney boats at it as well … Fishing the west coast was splendid … you were in among the islands and shelter. A good hour would put you into sheltered anchorage that you could hardly find your way out of in the mornings. *Alex Costie, Westray*

If you had a lot of fish to gut you couldn't leave the fish to go and get food, you had to get the fish cleared by, get them gutted and packed in ice … *Alex Costie*

You just worked at everything, the like of the boy that looked after the engines, he was up gutting on the deck, same as everyone else and whoever was doing the cooking, he knocked off to do the cooking but as soon as that was cleared he had to go up and gut fish as well with the rest.

We never went out before midnight on Sunday night because it was just the done thing at that time. There was no boats that went out before then, then we used to finish on a Friday … just after two or three years they started going out on a Saturday then a Sunday, just to gain an unfair advantage. That was when the rat race started.

Anon

At the seine net fishing, it was supposed to be a daylight fishing but guys like us that was in a hurry to get rich, or to get a deposit for a better boat would go inshore at night and fish for flatfish, you know, plaice, skate and that. We were inclined to work at both ends of the day which was geuy tiring really.

When we got another bigger boat, I preferred seine netting … There was no ice plants in Orkney at that time which was a bit of a nuisance and you had to make sure that you were in Wick or Scrabster at least once a week to get ice, sometimes we landed over there. Mostly we landed in Wick or Scrabster …

Sometimes in the summer we went to Aberdeen to land the catch which worked fine, just did weekly trips to Aberdeen At that time most of that class of boat was home at the weekend.

We continued landing in Wick or Aberdeen, sometimes we were just putting the fish in lorries and sending them to Aberdeen or Grimsby and over the years refrigeration got to be better and you got refrigerated wagons and after a while we got to land in Kirkwall. There was an ice plant in Stromness which we used some but years later when the ice plant came to Kirkwall it was very handy and we used to work a system of just landing in Kirkwall on a Sunday night or Monday and putting it into refrigerated wagons and sending it down to Aberdeen on the Tuesday.

Alex Costie, Westray

The tradition in Orkney has been share-fishing rather than wage earning that the east coast trawler crews have practised.

The pay was worked out, the expenses came off first then it was divided, half to the crew, half to the boat. *Anon*

It was divided two ways. One half went to the boat and gear and the other half was divided between the five o' a crew. When I first started you could do thirty or forty pound a week … If we got three hundred pound a week then each of the crew would get about twenty-five pound and a council worker at that time maybe only got eight pound a week. We were doing quite well … that was what we aimed for. I've seen a week or two at that time you'd get five hundred a week but there was many a time you just barely cleared your expenses so when it came to these kinds of things, we worked on kind of a sub, just hoping that the next week would sort of pull us out …

Alfie Sinclair, Stromness

Fishermen are paid almost entirely by what they catch. Sometimes it could be good, sometimes it could be disappointing. *Alex Costie, Westray*

The hard work and sometimes high earnings that came with working in the fishing went for some with hard drinking when back on shore. Dividing earnings between the crew in the bar often signalled the start of a weekend of drinking.

I worked out of Thurso for a lot years … There was the Marine Hotel just above the pier. On a Saturday you would get some of the skippers paying the men in the pub. That was never done on my uncle's boat. The money got divided up on the boat and you could please yourselves where you went after that. I thought that was a better way of doing it.

Alfie Sinclair, Stromness

It was good money [in the '80s]. You were eighteen or nineteen and sometimes you were earning nearly £30,000 a year. It was good … it's just got less ever since.

What did you do with the money at that age?

Oh, wasted it, spent it on drink.

Anon

Many a time you would be in the hotel and you might have had a few drinks beforehand but once you went down to the boat, that was it. You didn't go down carting drink with you.

On Sunday afternoon we took ice and headed out late on Sunday night to the fishing ground. You would land ten to twelve days later, then go straight back out and do it again. Sometimes you could work within an hour of the harbour, other times you could steam five or six hours. Other times, we were working the Butt of Lewis and it would take you eight hours to get there. No more than we had to.

Alfie Sinclair, Stromness

The seine net you only fish during daylight hours, because what you are doing is scaring the fish into the net and you lie at night … it depends on different times of the year but the summertime you are maybe getting up at four in the morning, getting to bed maybe at ten at night but you're on your toes all of that time but in the wintertime it's a cushy enough job, just nine to five, just like a shore job.

Anon

There were two winches and I was working one of the winches. Then the paths that they trawled were all marked out on their Decca machinery and they followed that and then when the nets were hauled and the fish came aboard it was sorted by species and size into different ponds on the deck and then the fish would be boxed up.

Julie Gibson, Rousay

You get up, shoot the net, then you'd have maybe an hour and a half before the first haul got taken on board so that would give you a chance to have your breakfast … you'd get your first fish on board then you'd finish working with that fish it was time to haul again. You were just on the go until your last haul on board.

It was like you worked eight on, four men home so the boat kept going the whole time. So you would do two ten day trips and then get home for ten days. When the [boat] came home she was single crew and there was just eight of us and we'd do two trips, then we'd get three days home … it was terrible. Then she went to crew and a half as well and it was six on, three off because there was less fish.

You would work in four hour spells, you would have two and a half hours to clear the fish, then you would have an hour and a half to do what you wanted, eat, sleep … you'd get a watch sometimes in that time as well … the longest you would ever get would be maybe three hours. You got used to it, sleeping in two hour spells rather than eight.

Usually the best doing boats would keep their crew. It was reasonably steady. It's no now, everyone just chops and changes now.

You had a steaming watch, when you were going home then basically you were just told to go from point A to point B and you'd make sure you did it without going into anything … towing watches, that's like when you are actually fishing, you more or less just had to follow a tow, like on a plotter. You just keep to the tow and make sure you didn't put the net into any wrecks … it usually came fast, that's when the net got stuck on the boat and you had to haul it back. Sometimes you canna get it back and you lose your net or tear your net and damage it … I don't think I've ever lost a net but I've certainly torn a net, I think everybody has really … maybe half of you would work to clear the fish and the other half of you would work to mend the net and basically you would get no sleep.

Usually the deeper you went the more you would see foreign boats, French and Spanish … Sometimes you would come into contact with gill netters … They basically just shoot miles of strips of just light netting which just lies on the bottom and the fish swim through and get trapped … If you met them there was always some trouble because you didna ken where their gear was and they couldn't speak English to tell you.

Anon

What kind of conversations go on between the boats?

Lies. Tell them you are not catching anything. Sometimes there is a bit of truth in there somewhere, based on a bit of truth. … to keep out of each others' roads you'd speak to each other. Sometimes you'd get boats that would pair off together and they would speak truthfully to each other, they would work private channels … Sometimes the skippers had radios at home but home couldna speak back to them but they would just give them a shout to say they were such and such a place and they would be home such and such a time. When you got closer to shore the phones started working again.

Anon

There were always radio conversations and the lies being told … skippers not telling each other the truth about what they were getting. It was always 'geuy fair' or 'really poor'.

Julie Gibson, Rousay

Since the Second World War fishing has been transformed. Technology has allowed boats to become bigger, their fishing potential to be much greater. They can explore deeper waters, stay away for longer and go out in all kinds of weather. Boats are now in constant contact with the shore and can talk to other boats using their radios. Radar has eliminated much of the danger presented by fog and now the Global Positioning System (GPS) means the exact location of the boat is always known. In the past, huge amounts of money have been made. The economic investment made by fishermen is so great that, now stocks are declining, they find themselves in serious financial trouble. A boat which is not catching to its potential can only run up debt. Grants and loans, which have been available since 1918 to help adapt and build new boats, are no longer available.

The size and catching power of the boats has increased enormously. The 'Orcades Viking III', a freezer trawler, the largest vessel in the current Orcadian fleet, is capable of landing a catch larger than that for the whole of Orkney in pre-war days. In 1997 the Orcadian fleet consisted of 189 boats with 402 fishermen (and occasionally women) working full- or part-time at sea. It seems likely that these numbers will continue to decrease, encouraged by decommissioning schemes from the Scottish Executive which aim to decommission twenty per cent of Scotland's whitefish fleet.

I think after the first generation of crew that we had they was young boys that had left school and gone straight into the fishing and when they grew up then, that lads were having boats of their own. The council began to give assistance for boats and that helped a good lot. We began to get a bigger and stronger class of boat … you had a greater continuity of earnings … bad weather didna affect you so much … and forbye that you were beginning to accumulate a lifetime o' experience … The nature of the seabed … what you could trawl over and what you couldna, where the wrecks were, the times of year you would get fish and as more and more local skippers had whitefish boats this information increased … during the seventies the whitefishing was booming around here.

It's only the crews that come from here now. Quite often the boats are no here from one month's end to the next.
Alex Costie, Westray

The *Orcades* in Stromness has more fishing power than the whole of the Orkney fleet in the herring fishing days and she is just one boat … the fish don't have a chance now …
Mungo Montgomery

I wouldna say I was concerned about that [about over-fishing]. Basically you are just hunting something … so you don't have much control over … when it becomes no longer economic to fish then you just won't fish … that's the bottom line … there have been times of scarcity and times of glut. When there is too many of them then you don't get much money for them which is no much use to you either … If you are catching nothing but big fish that's a very poor sign because there is no small fish coming up.
Alex Costie, Westray

There are four kinds of scallop in Scottish waters, two edible. It is the clam which is the main catch of scallop dredgers. Boats work with up to twelve dredges per side which rake the clams up from the seabed. This industry developed in Orkney in the 1960s. Boats which had towed nets were suitable for adaptation to clam dredging.

It was about the only job you could work with a small boat from Orkney, apart from the creels, and we weren't interested in the creels at all. The scallops is towing gear, same as a seine netter or a trawler so it was just what I knew really.

We travelled a bit more to Shetland and the West Coast. What really put us up to Shetland was the A.S.P.* and P.S.P.*, you ken, the shellfish toxins … Shetland was about the only place that was open for scallops … we were over a year there, just left the boats up there and flew home … some of them were fine and would speak away fine but the bulk of them didna speak to us at all.   *Anon*

*Amnesic Shellfish Poisoning, Paralytic Shellfish Poisoning

Sorting the catch on a scallop dredger

George Drever

WHALING

Whaling represented an opportunity for Orcadian men to earn good wages in return for spending a season in the harsh conditions of the polar sea. In the eighteenth and nineteenth centuries they were valued oarsmen on the Arctic whalers of Hull, Dundee and Aberdeen. During the twentieth century the main whaling grounds for British firms were in the Antarctic. Christian Salvesen & Sons of Leith was the main employer for Orcadians.

Two Salvesen factory ships operated in the Antarctic at the time; the 'Southern Harvester' and the 'Southern Adventurer'. Each factory ship had twelve catchers. The scale of the killing was enormous. William Sinclair's diary records the numbers of whales caught every day. Between the wars the number of blue whales visiting the Antarctic waters was around 150,000. Up to 29,000 blue whales alone were killed annually.

The industry had hunted the stock to near extinction when whaling stopped in the South Atlantic in 1963. Whaling was suspended in 1985 with an international moratorium.

A number of Orcadian men went to the whaling, including George Drever from Westray and his father, Samuel Drever. George Drever worked on the whale catchers as a wireless operator for four seasons. He also spent a winter in South Georgia, the whaling station, where they repaired and overhauled the boats. Conditions in South Georgia over the winter were grim, with basic facilities and appalling weather.

If a catcher came on a number of whales, they were supposed to report it so that others could join in, but they weren't always too keen on that, more concerned with their own catch.

You had a basic wage plus a bonus on the amount of oil that was produced. If you were on a catcher you were paid a bonus on the catcher's catch as well. Although it was all one expedition and you were supposed to co-operate, it was every man for himself in some respects.

They fired a harpoon with a line attached to it with an explosive head on it ... when they shot one they pumped air into it. If there was more around then you stick a flag on it and leave it drifting until you were ready to tow them back to the factory ... you could tow, I suppose half a dozen. The first catcher that was on their main job was towing in the whales from the other boats to the factory ship but we shot them as well ... The blue whale was the one they preferred because it was they were bigger ... There was a limit on the size of course ...

Communication was done in code. You didn't want to broadcast to everybody, what you were doing. There was over thirty other factory ships down there ... [from different companies] and different nations.

The early catchers that I was on there was no telephone. Your communication was entirely in Morse. The better

ones, the newer ones, they had telephone. It was wartime remember too and we were using wireless. It wasna really very sensible because the Germans sent a radar down there early in early 1941 and they captured three factory ships and a transport ship and there were ten or eleven whale catchers and took them back to France. So they got a good haul, a lot of whaleoil and fuel oil plus the ships.

We stopped using wireless to a great extent but I think it was too late, there was an armed merchant ship sent down then to look after us us but I think it was too late.

Alex Costie worked the 1960/61 season on the 'Southern Venturer', working the winches, pulling the whales on board the factory ships.

I had met a few men who had been whaling but not many ... I had been on leave, doing a bit of lobster fishing 'cause there was a seaman's strike in the Merchant Navy. I had been home about three months and that was about as long as you could stay without getting your call-up papers. Merchant Navy was a reserved occupation and if you weren'y in that you would have been called up for the army and that just was not an ambition of mine at all. So, at the end of the seaman's strike it was time for me to get a job. But when we got down to Leith all the seamen who had been on strike were looking for work and there was a shortage of jobs. Somebody said that Salvesen's were signing men on as whalers.

I thought it was a splendid job, the ship was good to work on, the quality of the men you were working with was a thousand times better than I had come across on my previous job which had been on a passenger liner ...

For a few days we took several sperm whales ... they weren't all that fussy about sperm whales, it was just to make sure everything was working. When the season really opened they were shooting fin whales and blue whales, mostly fin whales … The harpooners on board the catchers, that was their job … just like any men anywhere there were good ones and bad ones among them. Some of them had very few whales for the season and some of them had hundreds. Some of them were crazy men that chased whales in bad weather and got their legs broken with being washed off the gun platform.

I was working the steam winches, it was one deck up from where the whales and all the blood and the guts were. It was a cleaner job.

The rest of the carcass was heaved under the fore deck by people they called lemmers, they took the meat off it and separated off the bones and cut up the head into chunks that could be put down into the cookers. The meat was pulled further forward and cut up into chunks and put into a roasting plant …

Usually a tanker came down from this country and we would take fuel oil off the tanker and then the tanker would lie off again and wash out its tanks and stuff and then we would put whaleoil on board or bonemeal or whatever. You looked forward to the tankers coming down because you got a new film to watch.

We had to keep three or four bigger whales to use for fenders, you know between the two ships … even with that there was still too much motion sometimes and we had to go amongst the pack ice … it helped to flatten the sea … and you could pass over your stuff quite easily.

We had whale meat, once a week, just on Thursdays … we were picking just the very prime cuts and the Norwegians, the old whalers that were there, seemed to like it to hang for a week or two. It was fairly black on the outside but beautiful pink stuff on the inside … it doesnae taste oily, it's fine lean meat and the way they treated it was tender too … the Norwegians had plenty of good gravies to go with it. I looked forward to Thursdays.

We had salt meat a lot … I mind when I first gied aboard the whaler I really thought that salt junk was right good. We'd been lying around Shields and Leith for a while, drinking beer and this salt beef was just super but after two or three months I was so sick of it I couldn't eat it.

Factory ship 'Southern Venturer' during 1956/57 season

Photo: William Sinclair

Whales being cut up on board the factory ship *Southern Harvester*.

There was about everything you could think of, because you are down there in the Antarctic seas, there's nobody to repair anything for you, you've got to do it all yourself. So we had some very good engineers, turners and fitters and carpenters and electricians. Guys that would make whatever part of an engine you didn't have … It wasna just the engines of the factories you had to carry spares for, we had thirteen catchers to look after as well.

Some of them played ludo. You wouldna believe it, grown men playing ludo and getting into a right sweat and a temper about it …

I was in a cabin with a whaler that was quite good at carved whale's teeth, you ken, making penguins and that. So I spent some time trying to learn how to do that. That fairly passed the time.

There was no point in being homesick because you were doon there and there was nothing you could do about it. You were doon there to make money and you were busy getting on with that … The worst time that I found was when you had finished whaling, and you had nothing more to do and you just had to take the ship home, you knew it

Photo: William Sinclair

he catchers lined up in readiness for the season to open.

was going to take you a month. You just had to have patience and look forward to going through the tropics etc.

I thought it was a fine job. Fifty pounds was my total expenses and that was for sweeties and oilskins and that meant you had the rest of your pay ... that gave me the deposit on the first fishing boat I ever owned.

William Sinclair worked one season on the 'Southern Harvester' as a fifth mate in 1956/57.

Well there was that many folk spoke about it ... a lot of the Shetland crowd had been to the whaling and they said 'you should go' ... It was a big experience and nobody will ever go again, let's put it that way.

They were run like a mobile factory so you had the Captain, the Captain of the ship, they were in charge of the whole outfit ... they had nothing to do with the ship as far as running it from A to B ... they just looked over the whole thing and it was the Chief Officer who ran the ship. The Norwegian officers ran the Norwegian sections ... Everyone knew what they were doing.

You had the factory ship, that was the main ship, and you had maybe four or five hundred crew aboard to start with ... that ran twenty-four hours a day, it didna stop ... You had twelve hour shifts, everybody worked and then you'd send maybe two or three whale catchers out ahead of the factory ship, the rest of the catchers would hang about the factory ship when you started whaling ... Nobody wanted to move too far in case they came across whales ... they'd send out maybe two or three boats to look for whales ... they'd say 'We've seen twenty' then two or three catchers would shoot away after. Then they'd say 'we've seen six maybe fifteen mile to the south' and two or three would go down there ... There was great rivalry, but it wasn't a case of one catcher would get twenty whales and he wouldn't tell anybody because you couldn't shoot twenty whales, he'd maybe get three. It was far better to get another three or four whale catchers in and kill twenty than kill three and lose seventeen ... If there was only four or five whales then one bloke wouldn't tell nobody because he'd get them.

When they shot the whale, the whale was then pumped up with compressed air to keep it afloat, because a whale will sink ... a sperm whale doesnae sink, it will float but an ordinary fin or a blue or a humpback whale will sink so you had to pump air into them, then you put a buoy with a big pole and marker and a flag and a light and they had a beacon on them as well, an electronic beacon and we had what you call buoy boats ... They weren't catchers, you had two or three of them each expedition ... They were usually the older catchers and they went out and towed the whales in back. The actual whale catcher didn't tow them back, he didn't have time. He would just buoy them and shoot away for another two. Another boat would come and pick

up its whales ... All the whales were marked, they had a number for them, they came to the factory ship they were just hauled up and processed.

The factory ship was in the centre, roughly, of the operation ... You might have a whale catcher go away for two days you see, they might steam two or three hundred miles looking for them and they'd come back and say 'There is maybe fifty or sixty whales', ... We had to steam slowly because we had no steam, we were processing the whole time and the steam was the same as your engines so we had to steam down behind them and when you came down there were forty or fifty whales lying around ready to pick up.

These engines were steam ... At the time they were built ... 1946 ... they couldn't get diesels ... but the problem with the steam engines is that they were expensive to run

Whales used as fenders between *Sigfra* and another ship

Photo: William Sinclair

On board a whaling ship

but then they had advantages because all the processing plant was steam. You needed a heck of a power of steam aboard. Everything was steam. The factory was run on steam. But the trouble with it was that you were doing a lot of, what they call 'full cook', that was when the factory ship was up to one hundred per cent production. They had no steam for the engine and we had a big buoy boat and that would pull you along slowly.

Everything on a whale was processed. The only thing that wasn't processed on a whale was the guts. There was nothing else left ... it came aboard as a whale and ended up in a tank. You'd oil, from the blubber, then you'd whale meat which we had to process, it was dried and ground down into bags of whale meat, you'd bonemeal and you'd got a lot of the blood was processed into concentrate, you know like Bovril, it was concentrated down into a meat stock ... you used the head on a sperm whale and a friend of mine, he was what you called a bone saw man and he used to work this big steam saw ... and you would cut it and the oil that you would take out of that head was as clear, pure machine oil and ... it was just a sparkling oil ... they reckon the whale used to move this oil about its head, for balance.

There was a limit. You weren't supposed to kill a pregnant whale, you weren't supposed to kill a whale with a calf and you couldn't take them under a certain size ... if you did shoot one, then you didn't get paid for it anyway ... The gunners got a bonus for every whale you killed so there was no point in shooting a small whale because you didn't get paid anyway.

If they caught a pregnant whale and maybe there was a young one inside nobody spoke about that ... it was just dumped over the side ... that was the matter closed, there were no more remarks made. Usually the gunner that did that got a severe talking-to.

It was just rotten. Everybody smelt the same, that was the great advantage, you didn't smell anything because everybody smelt the same you were living in the smell of whale, cooking and steaming ...

Most of them [the Norwegians] spoke with a Shetland accent, a lot of them had Shetland words in their Norwegian. At one time I could speak quite a bit [of Norwegian].

The pay was good, you got a bonus for every whale that was caught, so much a ton.

From the time it came aboard the ship to the time it finished it took thirty to forty minutes. I mean it wasn't a day's work, it would be minutes ... it came up through the stern of the factory ship, it was phlensed there, that was cutting the blubber off, they were high paid, because they had to cut it like a banana, without damaging the flesh ... it came through this place they called Hell's Gate and it was just steam, smoke, blood. By the time it came through there the whale was peeled ... so then it was cut up into sections ... it never stopped, it moved the whole time through the ship ...

Well they had great big steam winches and when it came up onto the ship it was hooked onto a big claw like that and pulled up by the tail and as it moved ... the men didn't walk up and ... they just stood there, some of them got on top of it and they cut it, sliced it, another one stood on the deck ... it would come so far and they had wires underneath it and they would just turn it. I mean this is a hundred ton you're speaking about and they would just flip it over and crash and by the time it moved there was another one coming up ... it just went on the whole time ...

That ship was full of steam anyway, it was hot, when you were working on the ship, you were sweating ... you could touch the side of it on the deck and the deck was actually warm.

I think it was becoming obvious what was happening ... the British/Norwegian whaling boards controlled it fairly well but the Japanese and Russians ... they would shoot anything that moved ... it was really the Russians and Japanese that killed it off because we had a very strict limit ... you started on a certain date and you finished on a certain date ... you might be lying among a hundred whales and you couldn't touch them but the Russians and the Japanese would go down maybe a month before and stay a month or two after.

DIVING

Orcadians have not been slow in taking advantage of the potential to earn a living from diving. Sandy Robertson from Hoy worked as a linesman and then diver for Cox and Danks between the wars, raising the German fleet in conditions which would fill most modern divers with horror.

I got the chance to go as a diver's linesman … they didn't get paid-off as often. I got taken on as a dinghy wallah I was told 'When you're idle then go alongside the divers and watch what they do and learn the signals and I'll put you in for the first lineman's job that comes along'. So I took it. I did five year as a linesman … [you have to] listen and feel for [the diver's] signals. Four was his signal that he was coming up, four and one was 'stop', four and two was 'pull him up'. Double four was 'danger', then there were the signals for the crane … .

We started on the destroyers, a double row up by the Martello tower … When they started they didn't have a clue what they were doing … I think it took them six weeks or more to lift the first destroyer, well you see when we finished up we lifted three in a fortnight, then started on the big ships. It was new to everybody. The Italians had lifted a ship but they had lost a man a day doing it.

You can see what she looked like ready to come up and put the compressors on. About a minute and a half and you were sixty, seventy, eighty feet in the air.

If you were watching a man and he was all thumbs on top then he would be twenty times worse under the water. I could drill, tap, burn, weld, tighten guys, put up cleats. I could do it all before I went down. I got three pound ten a week when I started diving, big money. Of course you was a trainee, you know nothing, keep your mouth shut.

The divers were keen to get the linesman to go down because they knew what you had to put up with, to see what it was like, to know that if you pull anything you are only two or three pounds under the water and you can yank him all over the place with one hand.

Brass hat, a corslet and twenty pounds here and twenty pounds here and heavy boots … January in the slush and the sleet, your hands got cold. Two big woollen sweaters, two pair of pants, no, one pair was plenty, two pair of socks.

Most of us were young, thin and hardened grown, plenty of fresh air. You never got a bubble. The bubbles were for the fellas working in the ship, bad air. When you pushed the water down everything got rusty, the rust just swallowed the oxygen. You could go down in the morning with silver in your pocket and when you came up you looked at it and it was black. So what that did to your lungs I don't know.

We didna get any decompression chambers. You hung on the shot rope. Your first stop was forty feet, four, five minutes, seven or eight minutes at thirty feet, then double that at twenty and half an hour at ten feet. We used to arrange it so that half an hour was the full decompression. Five, ten and fifteen minutes and that was plenty hanging

on in cold water. Working on the bottom, we did in the morning or did that on the first part of the shift and got it over with and then you got up on a top part of the ship and then you were in fifty or sixty feet and finish off what you were doing then you could take your ordinary decompression …

You started work at eight o'clock here and by the time you got out by Cava it was nine and get your diving boat in position it was near ten then you went down, did two and a half hours, half an hour's decompression. Up twelve o'clock. All this boffins say we didn't do a second shift. Oh yes we did. We were working for a private firm that was looking for profit. We went down and did a second shift.

Since the Second World War an interest in diving for pleasure has introduced many people to diving but a few have made it their living, scrapping from wrecks, repairing and maintaining ships and providing diving holidays for diving clubs. Anthony Duncan started diving on wrecks for scrap and, in the early 1980s, started one of the first businesses providing holidays for diving clubs.

It cost sixty pounds at that time for a bottle and we made our own suits, a snorkel, a mask and a knife and that's all we had. I went up to Stromness to the pool. They said this is what you have to do and I was a good swimmer so I did it all. No lectures on how much weight to use or anything else. So we started off with far too much weight but we gradually reduced it by about half. We just used to do shallow dives, around the barriers.

Davey Gorn that was diving at that time and John Finlay and one or two others, it was just talking and 'Look out don't do this' and 'Watch out for that'. That was the way it was learnt. The first time I went in deep sea was diving off a wreck off the east coast of Burray and B had found this wreck and it had red lobsters and we went off to have a dive on it too … It was my first dive, about thirty feet, beautiful and clear, the wreck was lying there, I was just fascinated. I was so fascinated, I ran out of air. I got to the surface, but I had so much weight, this forty pound of weight that I couldna keep me head up, I had no snorkel at that time and I shouted for help but they were that busy hauling in scrap with the hauler they never heard me so there was no way I could swim with all that on so I let go of my weight belt. That's the only time I ever did that. I

Anthony Duncan in the wheelhouse of the *Shalder*

Photo: Courtesy of Anthony Duncan

Mostly the Barriers … sometimes we would go further afield. We had a small thirteen-foot wooden speed boat and we had been looking at the charts and there was a wreck on the east side of Flotta, S54 and it was First World War German ship and it broke loose in a storm and it had been forgotten about and so the two of us went to look for it. We threw over an anchor where we thought it was, it was close inshore and over we went and it was there. The ship was all broken up and it was like being in heaven, there was so much copper pipes …

got back as white as a sheet. It gave me hell of a fright, and said 'I had to ditch my weight belt'. 'Oh go back and get it' was all I got. And anyway they went back and got it. Forty pound of lead was a big loss at that time.

After a few dives we realised that we were on a gold mine. We had sixty cubic foot bottles and we used to drive down to the Barriers and the best we got was forty-two pounds a hundredweight for one dive. The wages then was ten pound so diving was very profitable. Some of the other boys went for scallops in the Bay of Firth and what they did, they would dive during the weekend and maybe one or two nights per week or maybe more, doing a job besides and with doing that they could employ four or five tradesmen to build their house and that paid for it. We were on the scrap which was the same but different … They used a lot more bottles than what we did. You was talking ten, fifteen feet and they would maybe use three or four bottles but we gradually got that we would use two in an evening.

Scrapping is awful heavy work. You only had a small boat to work with and everything was carried up the beach, taken home and any iron was taken off it. You had to do it right away. You could leave it maybe two days but if you left it a week the iron went hard and it rusted and every bolt was a battle to get it off. If you do it when it comes out of the sea it was effortless …

Sport divers preparing to explore wrecks in Scapa Flow

We got a pattern and a roll of neoprene and we cut it all out then we stuck it together with glue and the next night we would try it on and it was baggy here and we cut it again until it was tight and then we'd sew it and put a tape on the outside … I had it for years … we was working on wrecks and we were always getting them torn and we were young, we didn't feel the cold.

We tried to stay shallow, we could stay down for a long time. We knew we wouldna get the bends, we knew we were safe.

I've seen us taking a porthole home and getting a two-pound hammer and smashing the glass out of it and selling it for scrap then, years later, we did scuba diving and everybody wanted a porthole and we'd smashed them.

… we had to diversify and do something else. There was a dive magazine … I had just built a new boat and we had the property and so it all worked together … we sent a letter to all the clubs. The first year we had seven parties and the next year we were fully booked … there's nowhere else you dive like that.

More recently the divers have been able to earn a living through diving for clams and occasionally spoots and other shellfish. They are unique amongst fishermen in that look for their catch under the water. Gary Miller came to Orkney on a diving holiday but returned to make a living diving for clams around Orkney.

I had been working in Coventry and I had been there eight years and it was getting to the stage where I didn't enjoy it because, well, the job you did, they wanted any old crap turning out and it wasn't the way I was taught like. … I applied for me redundancy … I was up here on holiday and I realised I didn't really have anything to go back for so … the Friday night was like a night out and I managed to find myself a job and a place to stay.

… I knew what a scallop was and I could dive so I used to dive off the boat when we weren't at the creels and get a few scallops, that's how I got into that.

When you work on boats, on the creels and that you kinda work a share, like. It could be half to the boat and half to the crew so you are on a quarter share, you find out what you're going to get before you go on a boat … it was only averaging about a hundred pounds a week you know, which was rubbish … we were going out of Kirkwall and there was two fellas diving off another boat for clams, or scallops and their boat broke down so they had asked this fella if they could come and dive off his boat. I was doing a bit of diving off the boat and they come on the boat and we went diving. They knew some of the good bits and give

you a few pointers, you know, so I was diving and they had telt us when you dive. It's just a thing that happens up here when you dive for clams they belong to you and you sell them and then you give the boat a share. You give them a quarter share of whatever you make. That was the best money I had made then, since I had come to Orkney so the fellas on the boat said, 'you will only get better at it' so I went with them.

In some bits you find them really close together, other bits they are spread out, you get them on sandy bits, you get them on stony ground, you get them in tide, you get them in bays, you just cannot say … You try and figure it out, where they'll be but you cannot.

If you're swimming along and they are sitting facing you it looks like a big smiley face and they are really easy to see but if they are shut and they've got a bit of weed growing on them and if they're closed in they just blend in with the bottom. … if they are open you can pick them up easy enough but what makes your money is the ones that are shut.

Over a period of years and you're diving the same bit of ground it suddenly clicks into place. How you find the clams on that piece of ground best, maybe a certain distance off the seabed, maybe facing into the tide and drifting backwards. It finally clicks into place. Even though you don't speak about it with the other divers you find out that over a period of time they've learnt exactly the same as you … you might be having a bad week, it happened to me. I was finding it hard, for one reason and another, things weren't coming right and we were diving on a bit that [another diver] had been diving on for years and he knew it inside out. Just before I jumped over the side he said 'What you need to do is get reet doon, with your nose right in among the sand and approach it from different angles and then you'll see them' … I just did what he said. It might have taken me another three or four years to find that out meself.

Because it's gone on for a good number of years in Orkney there are certain bits where you know they gather … and you kind of get to learn them … when you move on a different boat you kinda learn off the fellas. You just fancy somewhere, you have a try here and a try there. Sometimes you drop on the seabed and it's kind of barren and you'll come up and other days you hit it right. … sometimes you can hit it lucky, where nobody has ever been before and you always remember. What you do is take marks on the land, you know, like … you'll kind of put two houses over each other, if there are two houses on a hill there's a house at the top of the hill and a house at the bottom and they are maybe over each other and then at ninety degrees you'll take another mark, maybe a mast over a farm. That's how you get to know your spot on the sea and you'll always remember that. If you have a good picking of clams and you make money from it you mind them marks on and then maybe after a year you go back and have another look there.

With modern GPS you can just put a marker on and you can always get back there again or when you come to the surface you take a land mark. That's what we all dae because we don't want anyone else to know, so you take marks and you've got them in your head and they're yours then …

Across the broad of your hand is about four inches and the minimum landing size for clams is four inches. So when you are reaching for stuff if it is covered by your hand then it is too small.

Normally you only do three dives a day. Years ago, before the days before computers and dive tables, fellas used to do dive after dive but that's when they got into trouble and got bent.

You have a net bag. You make an entrance out of alcathene, everybody had their own little ways with their bags and then you have a line tied to your bag with a dan tied to the other end. Obviously that goes to the surface so that the boat can follow you.

Sometimes you go apart but the fella will just keep an eye on you … then you have a two gallon container tied to your bag as well, with a big hole it so that when your bag gets heavy you squirt a little bit of your air in and it takes the weight and as you put more clams in your bag you put more air in, that's what we call the lifter. It takes the weight of your clams so you can fin about the bottom with it.

Some fellas have two dans, a trailing dan so that you don't get mixed up with creels buoys if you are working in among creels so the fella on the boat knows which dans belong to which divers and if the divers do get too far apart then the fella on the boat … he would … motor the boat over to them and bang on the ladder with a big hammer … and the fella on the bottom can hear that and it's a signal that we all know and he will come up then and he can get him moved back … it doesn't go doon well because normally the one who's far apart he is getting a good picking and when he hears the chapping on the ladder he does not want to come up … but you always have to come up like, even if they are thick.

There will be a few of you on the boat and sometimes you come across a good bit so you put them all in your bag and then you'll be coming to the end of your dive and you'll still be seeing clams on the bottom and it might be good and they are pretty thick and you're thinking 'Good it's time to come up but me next dive I'm going to do alright', and you are sitting on the boat and you have two or three bags each and you leave that bag and of course it attracts a bit of interest and they'll say 'How are you getting on?' not wanting to ask you too much and you'll say 'not bad, you know', you don't want to say they are thick because you

Gary Miller, clam diver, Scapa Flow

know that on your next dive you'll have visitors, you know. They'll not drop on where you are diving they kind of find their way there you know. If you haven't been doing very well, well you want to give them room to work but you want a few clams you know. You normally find your way there … it's the tide you know, it takes you there, canna do nowt about that.

It's a bit of a pain when you are on them and somebody's edging on but you canna do nowt about it but you divna mind really because you are all pals anyway. You want everybody to make a living but you're not selfish … you divna want all the clams … you want everybody to make a picking, get good day's pay … you know, keeps everybody on the boat happy.

You always get one or two fellas who are noted for picking up lobsters … you've got to winkle them out of their little crevices, there's kind of a knack to it, getting them oot, some lads if they come across one they'll get them oot. If you are getting good money for them they'll sell them but for most folk it's like a treat, they'll just eat them … Now and again people will pick up a crab, if they fancy crab for their tea.

What we have done in the past is got in contact with a fella up in Shetland and gone up there and dived from his boat in Shetland, which is like a holiday you know. It's a good carry on that, getting away … it's a pain in some respects because you've got to make more money but all the time we've been away we've done alright. You see different places, meet different folk. Normally, wherever you are diving, you get a bit of a frosty kind of reception, well obviously, from other fishermen but there's not that much diving for clams goes on in other areas so, once you've stayed there for a while, you've maybe pointed out to some fellas lost creels or stuff like that they get to know you and they get to accept you a bit better.

You canna put your finger on it. You'll speak about it, you try and learn as much as you can and that's what you do, speak about it the whole time. You never, ever suss it out. You think there'll be stuff here and stuff there … [you watch where the other boats go] as best you can, and watch what they land as well, oh aye, you've got to, it's in your interest.

You got to keep your options open now in the fishing, especially now with the clams bans coming on and stuff like that.

What you find with the clams with most folk, it's not just a job. You dae it because you like it. That's why I'm doing it, because I like it. That's what takes you through the bad times as well … You find a lot of folk like wildlife, it's not just diving and picking up clams, you see a hell of a lot of wildlife you know and you like being on a boat and the freedom that goes with it.

Seals, you get them the whole time. They are a right pain … they always seem to have a thing about your fins and they always come up behind you and it's a bit unsettling,

when they are behind you. You'll be trying to shoo them away and they are coming up behind you pulling your fins because they have a thing about fins. They never bother you except when it's about October-time and it's pupping time and the bulls will try and intimidate you, they just come storming past you, barking, but there's nothing going to bother you, there's nothing to bother you in the sea unless you bother it.

The ones when we don't like when we are diving are what called lion mane jelly fish with the tentacles coming off, especially in tide. You'll dive in tide and then you'll come up your line and sometimes you might gan into what you call decompression when you have to stop at ten feet for a few minutes before you can come to the surface, you'll slip up your line then and you might be in a little bit of tide then you'll be hanging on your line, waiting for your computer to clear and tell you you can gan to the surface and you get these lion mane jelly fish drifting down, you have to keep and eye on them because the tentacles get round your face and any bit they can sting. Its not bad like but some folk take it bad … makes your face tingle for hours.

Most folk have training these days because anyone can dive, you just get your gear on and jump in the water, it's when something goes wrong, that's when you need your training. At the clams it's minimal equipment … if something fails you just have to rely on your training to get you out of whatever situation. Just two month ago I was diving … it was the first dive of the day and I just dived over the side, one hundred and forty feet of the water and I can't remember what depth I was, I didn't feel comfortable in me suit and I kind of shrugged my shoulders and the zip split and the cold water just rushed in, well it just takes your breath away and you lost your bouyancy as well, you've just got to keep your cool, I just grabbed me line and pulled meself up.

Now if you are deep in the cold water your valve can freeze and you can feel ice crystals form in your valve and it can freeze … most of the modern valves when they freeze they go into free flow so you can still get a breath of air …

I don't know what that would feel like, folk coming up and 'poaching'. You'd kind of think that. It's different when we go away, it's us poaching you know. I mean it's one of those things, you have to do it for a living. What are we supposed to do? Ideally we would fish here, we wouldna want to go and fish on someone else's ground but you've got to make a living. What you wouldn't want is folk coming up and damaging the fishing here, like taking the small stuff and really hammering an area.

Then you are working for yourself. You've got naebody to say do this do that, you please yourself … that's the good thing about diving, you're all self-employed. If you didn't want to go to work then you don't go to work … if you fancy a day off you have a day off. If you only fancy doing one dive … it's however hard you want to work …

'Nearly all the seagoing people at the time, from Orkney and Shetland went to the *Dolphin*. You had to get some kind of training course first so the *Dolphin* was the one you went to and you were there eight, nine months and if a job came up you went. You just learnt general seamanship, what to do, rowing, sailing, that sort of thing . . .'

William Sinclair

MERCHANT NAVY

Joining the Merchant Navy was often the easiest way to fulfil ambitions of an adventurous life at sea. Orkney has a long tradition of the men spending years away in the Merchant Navy. It was a hard, sometimes isolated life, away from family for long periods of time. Compared to local wages at the time, the money was good and it was often enough to give men capital for boats or businesses on their return.

You could join the Merchant Navy at sixteen, as an Ordinary Seaman, and then, after three years sea-time you became an Able Seaman. An alternative was to join at a much lower wage as an apprentice but with the prospect of becoming an officer after some study. If you wanted to progress through the ranks, you had to pay for your own expenses while studying between trips. You could also join as a carpenter or an engineer, if you already had a trade.

Men found work through word of mouth or by utilising contacts from home or through the seamen's homes. Every major port had a seamen's home, often run by religious organisations which offered seamen a place to stay between voyages.

There were of course ways of supplementing your income for those who were not afraid of taking some risk. Buying cigarettes or electrical items in one country to sell in another was a way of earning more money.

Since he [my son] was a child, long before he started to go to school … he was talking about going to sea and I really did try to discourage him. I thought 'Oh, it's a hard life'. He kept on and on and on. One time, when he was maybe about six or seven and the *Ola* hadn't crossed the Firth because the weather was bad, but you know there are times when you can slip across the Firth, even on a bad day. So Stephen, Ian's father, he and Willie Mowatt were going out to put a man who was desperate to get back, onto the mainland. They were going to slip across at a certain time and tide and I allowed Ian to go on this trip and it was wild. I was sick all the time, thinking what a shameful thing it was to do. I thought this would cure him of his passion for the sea and it was mother who was ill all the time they were away … When he came back, he comes in, cheeks aglow, happy, smiling. He had enjoyed every minute of it. At the end of the day I had to say 'if that's what you are going to do … '. When he was thirteen he was on about it again. I said that if he was going to go then he could go on an old Aberdeen trawler and he said 'Yes, if that's the only way I can go to sea, that's what I'll do'. After that I didn't try to actively discourage him but I knew that's what was going to happen. *Helen Manson*

I never had any other thought in my head, I was just desperate to get to sea, deep sea, as an apprentice.

Robin Dennison

The only thing I wanted to do was to go to sea. There's an old man, old John Hourie, he said 'If you are going to sea lad then get on the coast first, good training' so that's what I did. *Willie Tulloch*

Fishing here at that time was just small lobster boats, a summertime job. There wasnae many folk, indeed just about nobody did it over the winter and a lot of my friends were in the Merchant Navy. *Alex Costie*

I think most that went to sea had some seafaring background, their parents, you know brothers or family that went to sea. It's something like farming. There's some relation in the farming. There's very few folk who actually come straight into farming from something completely different. There's usually some link. You mostly found that if they were from the islands, from Orkney or Shetland, there was either fishing connections or Merchant Navy connections in the family. *William Sinclair*

I went to the School of Navigation in Southampton … and I stayed there for a year. We marched up and down with rifles above our head. That's mostly what we did down there. We got navigation in the morning but the rest was drill … Obeying orders was the great thing … by the time I went on my first ship, if I had been told to jump over the side by an officer, I would have done it without question. *Robin Dennison*

They used to post up on the noticeboard jobs that were coming up … Companies that were looking for apprentices or deck boys or cadets. When you came sixteen, then you could apply for a job. You could start looking … who was taking apprentices … If you were going on deck, you had to apply to the Shipping Federation, the pool they called it, then they took you on their books and, if a job came up, they'd get in touch with you at the *Dolphin*. *William Sinclair*

I left when I was seventeen, I wanted to see the world. They weren't very keen about it, they thought I was too young to go away. I thought otherwise . . . I just felt I wanted to go.

. . . I wanted to see how much of the world I could see. My mother had a relation in a high job in a company, Donaldson's Shipping Company, and he wrote to say there was a berth free and if I came now I could have a job on a ship . . . It was a big adventure going away. I had never been out of Orkney before I went on the boat to Leith and this friend, a lighthouse keeper's son who was at college in Edinburgh met me and I was right glad to see him standing on the pier, I can tell you.

The first job I did was cleaning the water tanks on the ship and there was no electric lights on the ship so we had candles. It took two or three days to clean this tank with the old cement wash and filled with water and we sailed. It was a gale of wind, you see, a west wind, we were going down the Clyde, about five o'clock, tea time and we and this other young lad and me were in the mess room and these old fellas said 'Now boys, take a right feed while you're at it because you'll no eat for another week', and that was about the size o'it. Came out of there, and it was rough. It took us a fortnight to reach Montreal and I was sick . . . I said to myself that if I am still alive when I get back to Glasgow I am going home. We had a bad passage on the way back but the wind was behind us and I didn't want to go home, couldn't have cared less then . . .

There was always a man to wheel in they days, two hours at a time. Night time there was a man to the wheel, a man on lookout in the crow's-nest . . . a thing like a barrel way up the mast, stood up there all night, an hour at a time, sometimes two, depends which watch you are on. It was very cold up there. The wind blew down, hit the bottom of the crow's-nest and blew up under your clothes, blown out through your neck . . . It was a big job up there in wintertime, in bad weather or sometimes in fog. That's the only ship I've seen with a crow's nest . . . If the weather was moderate you would stand in the bow for your hour, two hours, watching for shipping you see.

When you go in as an apprentice you get little or no pay. I got the chance to go as an apprentice and pay was twelve pound in the year and you had to buy a uniform for sixteen pound so you were out of pocket to start wi'. Any kids with parents who had money could afford to do that. Right on to the end of four years, maybe in the last year they would get twenty pound a year and then, if they can't pass for officers, they are worse off than the Ordinary Seaman . . . In the depression an awful lot of folk had tickets, Captain's tickets and had to work as an Ordinary Seaman. On one ship I sailed on all the A.B.s had tickets, even Captain's tickets among them.

You got a discharge book and every time the ship comes back to Glasgow you sign off, you get paid off and you

stamp your book, 'Good behaviour', things like that . . . and then you signed on again next time . . . when you go to look for a different ship they want to see your book and if it's a good clean book you get your job, that's how they track anyone. If someone goes to another country and jumps ship, never came home with the ship, that's a bad discharge and it's hard to get a job after that. You must be prepared to come back.

In London I went to the sailors' home . . . It was just like a hotel, wee rooms, single bedrooms. Full board. Before the war it was twenty-one shillings so you could stay there a while . . . and you were quite well fed . . . across the road was what they called the Shipping Federation and that was the folks who looked for the men for the different companies and a man would come over into the home and he wa say ' I'm looking for six men, or eight men. A.B.s, wanted now. If you are interested come over'. So we went over and stood in this wee room and they'd stick their head out and say 'A.B.s books please' and in most cases that I've I got a job, no bother. But there was a whole load of fellas there who didn't have a book discharge, only what they call a paper discharge, it's just no use then . . . they mostly worked in the small boats up and down the coast . . . and they wouldn't get a job in the big boats. You wouldnae get a job without a book.

Every time you go away and come back on a trip on a ship, you pay off, you can either sign on again or just try a different ship, say crossing the Atlantic. In the wintertime of the year it's no good. Like bad days in Orkney the whole time so I'd be looking for a ship going east you see . . . I like going east, through the Mediterranean . . .

Jimmy Groat

You had to watch what you said. You couldn't have been too far or say you had done too much . . . it was resented. I remember making the mistake of saying how bad it had been on the first two years. I got a lot of digs about that . . . Years later I was having a drink with a local man, who had been at sea all his life, and he had been on the same run and I said to him, 'When I was away I saw more bad weather in six weeks than I saw in six years in the Indian Ocean. Did you no find that?' 'Oh yes, but don't come home here and say that'.

I wanted to go to sea . . . Everyone had done the same thing. My father had gone to sea as a carpenter. I just wanted to do the same thing I suppose. I went down to Newcastle and got a job out of there as a carpenter on the Stag Line . . . She was a light ship and she was an old Liberty ship and she was red rusty. The propeller was half out of the water and oh my God, what an ugly looking thing. What we did afore we left, they pumped about seven feet of water in number five hold before we left and that took her propeller down in the water and we went across that Atlantic in that and roll? You've no idea. It was a six week trip and every six weeks they had to have a new crew. Not one came back. I didn't realise ... I thought it was my first job at sea and I'd better not lose it, I might not get another carpenter's job. I stuck it for two years. It was pure hell.

I always say that I saw more bad weather in six weeks in the Atlantic than I saw in six years in the Pacific. It was terrible.

... I've seen a week that we couldn't go on deck but I didn't have experience. I though it was just normal. After I had been on other ships I thought 'Hell's bells I'm never going back there' I should have twigged on. Nobody else was staying on.

They called the Stag Line, Orkney's Navy. It was a Stromness man, Harvey, that was Superintendent. He took away all the Orkney ones. John Hourie used to have a steam ship that used to come to Burray pier for sand to take to Lyness, gave them hand, shoveling so they gave me a glowing reference.

I was on tremendous wages at that time. I was on about forty pounds a week and I came home and I was on ten pound a week . . . a good wage then was about eight pounds a week.   *Anthony Duncan*

That ship was going round the world the whole time. We did four trips round the world on her in two years so it was a good way of getting around ... I joined that ship in

Galveston and we went from there to China and Japan and then we loaded cargo and came back round to America, New York, Baltimore and all them places, Philadelphia, St John's Halifax, then we loaded cargo again on the American coast and back again across to Japan, China, Shanghai, Hong Kong, Singapore . . . the trip took roughly about four months. We were based in America . . . we took mainly rubber, foodstuffs, general cargo from Japan. We loaded chromium ore, that was very high grade for making stainless steel, we took that to America. We had copper . . . we carried coconut oil, that ship had tanks on board, maybe two thousand ton of coconut oil . . . when the ship was loading you were on duty the whole time . . . places you went to you were loading twenty-four hours a day . . . the docks worked twenty-four hours a day and we worked our shifts.

You went ashore at any opportunity, clear off the ship. Everybody went off the ship as fast as they could. Usually you were fed up by that time. You maybe take about six weeks across the Pacific and by the time you got there you were fed up, everybody was desperate to get off.

There were about eight white crew and and about forty Indians. Different companies took them from different areas. You might get all your crew from Calcutta, some of the them took them from Goa, some of them from Bombay, some were Ceylonese ... this company had quite a few Maldive Islanders . . . they were good seamen, they were brought up by the sea.

You did your correspondence courses as an apprentice but after that it was just up to yourself whether you went for your next tickets ... it was a minimum of three months at school but usually it was five ... at that time there was a lot of colleges ... Aberdeen, Glasgow ... it got your brain going because at sea you kind of stagnated and then you decided, 'right, I am going now for a Second Mate's ticket' so you had to think 'right, I am going to work now' . . . get your whole act together . . . Nobody paid you very much . . . you had to save up . . .   *William Sinclair*

The thrill was gone. Every port's the same. I've been there and done it. I have no desire to go on a cruise or go anywhere foreign. I would far rather go up with a sail to one of the islands or go fishing. That's my idea of heaven.
                                        Anthony Duncan

Photo: Courtesy Anthony Duncan

Anthony Duncan relaxing with crew on the *Aukland Star* in Timaru, New Zeland

Robert Gillespie of Pow and James Munro of Breval, repairing a boat at Breval, Rousay

BOAT BUILDING

There is a long tradition of boat building in Orkney. The Orkney yole is descended from the Norse 'yolle' boat, adapted to meet the tidal conditions in Orkney. Many people have built boats out of interest, as a natural extension of their love of the sea. There are identifiable styles for the small dinghies and yoles which originate from each of the islands. These are supposed to be connected to the use to which they were put and to the kind of seas they were likely to encounter. The North Ronaldsay pram is a good example of adapting ideas for local conditions. The first pram was made in the 1920s at Milldam by Hughie Muir Shoultisquoy and Willie Cutt. The design was taken from a Norwegian boat. Although it had twice or thrice the creel-carrying capacity of the flatties which were still in use, the new pram had more buoyancy and greatly improved seaworthiness, free from drag and far lighter to row than any skiff or yole. Its high stern made it very suitable for lobster fishing and beach landing.

… each area had their own type of boat and that was the best kind of boat that you could get … North Ronaldsay had their prams, and there was the Stroma yole and the Swona yole.   *Mungo Montgomery*

There wasn't desperate much difference …The skiffs which were in the North Isles were narrow and long. The boats in the Pentland Firth tended to be much wider craft. There was good reason for this. The direction that they were required to sail was across the sea, rather than with the sea and quite a lot of the North Isles boats just sailed to sail out against the swell and back in with the swell but the South Isles; South Ronaldsay, Swona, Stroma and the Caithness coast, you needed an entirely different boat which could take the same size of sea over the side as what it could take over either end.   *Cyril Annal*

Most of the fishermen used to [paint] their own but as the years went on people wanted to go on holiday so they would just take the boats up and leave them for you to paint them … it got more as time went on. You just had a bucket and scrub it then sand it down by hand.

Robin Duncan

The wood of course had to be steeped before it could be bent. It was put in one of that ditches that goes by Milldam. Running water you see and stones put on it to make it bend. It is much easier to make them leaner for you don't have to make it do this bending.

The Kirk Taing at certain times, you get a north tide, it makes that much disturbance you'd think that you were in a pot boiling and then the sea would be as high as that door, at least three feet higher than the bow of the boat and you just had to keep steering …and that is where your fullness counted besides leaness. That old boat at Waterhouse [built in North Ronaldsay] was exceptional in those circumstances. Where she canna go I wouldna like to be.   *John Cutt, North Ronaldsay*

At one time most islands had their own boat builder but now there is only one professional boat builder in Orkney; Ian Richardson in Stromness. Duncan's boatyard was run by the same family for four generations and represented a tradition going back centuries until it closed in 2001. Originally the work they did was with wood and clinker-built boats although recently they worked with most modern materials. Their reputation as skilled craftsmen was considerable.

They burst a stem … the Shetland fellas were saying you'll need to get it repaired and they said we'll just bolt it together and we'll take it down to Jimmy Duncan's in Burray and they beached it down at the burn, down here and the only time he could get to it was at low water. He went down, took a measurement and went back up and, during the time of one tide, he made a new stem and then went down fitted it and they were away on the next tide. It took some doing, one man to do that.

Mungo Montgomery, Burray

James, Anthony and Robin Duncan working together in Duncan's boatyard, Burray

Photo: Robin Duncan

It's a hell of a start in life. If you can build a boat, a house is no problem ... I always felt it was tremendous advantage. You weren't frightened to try something new ... It is a tremendous apprenticeship. You learn a bit of engineering, a bit of metal work, boat work, woodwork. If you can do that and build a boat then there are very few jobs you canna tackle.   *Anthony Duncan*

You started off by watching what my father did, what my grandfather did and they explained it as you went along. Not like noo where you get modules ... they've got it all on paper and not in the hands.

Duncan boats are known. Now, a lot of people can just look at a boat and say 'It's a Duncan boat'. It gives you a bit of satisfaction when you can see what your father's done and your grandfather's done. It's never been a money making thing ... as someone said to me 'You let your heart rule your head'. But I get a lot of satisfaction out of it. You see something at the end of your life.

The first three planks you put on, if they're not right, then your boat's wrong ...

The quickest we ever did a thirty-six footer that was twelve weeks and that was good going that.

Most boats had to be built light because people didn't have the slipways and that to take them up wherever they could so they hadn't to be made too heavy and as time went on, the facilities got better and they got heavier ...

We were in the small concrete shed. There was electricity from a generator, just ran at night. We had a circular saw driven by a diesel engine. Everything else was done by hand. No machinery, no power tools and then power came in, before 1955, because the first thing I remember getting was an electric drill and that was marvellous, instead of boring everything by hand ...

We did everything. We did joinery work, we could mend a cart, we were the local undertakers. We made coffins ... You just more or less had to do everything that was connected with wood. I'll give you an example. This house we are in now, my father and grandfather built it and the one in front of that ... they built a whole lot of houses ... that was in the thirties when things were a bit quiet.

I could make a window but I had to think a lot ... Boat building is entirely different from ordinary joinery work because there is very little that is made plumb or square ... I find it difficult with joinery work, you know, when you are having to plumb everything off, square it off. I can do it, but it takes me a while, whereas if something is crooked or off the plumb, that comes just no bother at all. *Robin Duncan*

When James Duncan started his apprenticeship, steam trawlers and drifters from the east coast would have mingled with locally made dinghies and yoles, some still working with sails, others with engines fitted. Now boats are fitted with diesel-driven engines generating electricity to work fish-finding and navigational systems. Boats have become bigger and materials have changed. Equipment and materials for fishing are no longer made locally or by the fishermen themselves but are bought in from specialist manufacturers. Accommodation on board boats has improved and most are now fitted with toilets and washing facilites.

None of the fishing boats had toilets … what you call bucket and chuck it. All the seine net boats … the toilets they would have had … the first marine toilets were just fitted in by the engine room alongside the fuel tank. There was no separate toilet. The first fishing boat that we would have fitted a toilet in would have been in the 1970s.

We could only take up a boat of about twenty-odd feet. Can't take anything bigger than that. Someone on either side of the boat and you just literally pulled it up the beach [we] greased the wood with tallow or soft soap. If you had old greenheart you didn't need to grease because it is slidey as it is. If they had a wheelhouse you couldn't get them through the door. It always made it a bit more awkward.

The type of boat building we did was all by the look of the eye and I always think if it looks good to the eye it's right but if there's something that's wrong you can just see it … I don't know if I'd got a good eye or not but I used to be able to pick things out.

You would say 'I want a boat that is so many feet long, so wide and whether it is a stern cruiser or what', and you were more or less left with that. He would tell you what sort of engine he wanted in. He would say 'put the wheelhouse there'. That's how it went on. There were no plans.

We never did [any decoration]. I know fishing boats had what they call a cove line put in and you know they painted a sort of gold colour with an arrow head at one end and arrow feathers at the other or fancy curls. It was just purely decorative. We never bothered with all that. People didn't want to spend the money out. Unless it was functional it wasn't done.

We used to get mostly oak and larch. You would specify logs x number of feet long and specified what you wanted it cut to and they just cut the log and banded it together and you actually got the whole log home … Nearly all the larch was Scottish. You can get Russian larch or European larch but it doesn't seem to work as well, doesn't bend as well.

One chap used to come up from Edinburgh to install the radio and Decca did the radar … Now electronics are much simpler.

There'd be no safety equipment. I remember the first lot of boats we did under the loans and grants, we did a quote for the life-raft and you'd get the quote back 'Please remove the life-raft' because they'd save maybe a couple of hundred pound. It was only when a boat sank between Barra and the mainland and they found three fish boxes tied together … in that days it would have been before the M.C.A.* came in that was when they started making the rule a boat of a certain size had to have a life-raft. It became compulsory to have life-jackets, lifebelt, flares, life-raft, first aid kit, fire bucket, fire extinguishers, gas detector, bilge detector, escape hatches out of the accommodation, horns, radar reflectors and all that had to go on. But they could only make it compulsory when something had happened. Originally people only wanted a very basic boat. If they could sail it away, that was it.

At one time they used to put an engine right in the middle because they reckoned it balanced in the boat. Now they can have them anywhere they want … The majority of the people in the north working creels prefer the wheelhouse as far forward as they can fit to give them space aft. A lot of the ones down south put their wheelhouses right aft and leave all their space forward. If the wheelhouse is aft then it is the most comfortable because it goes up and down less.

Robin Duncan

Boats are never big enough in the water and too big out of the water.
Mungo Montgomery

Fibreglass boats began to be introduced in Orkney in the 1960s and for a time were manufactured by Halmatic at Hatston Industrial Estate in Kirkwall. The first fibreglass boat designed for commercial fishing was designed and built at Hatston and fitted out at Duncan's boatyard in 1972.

A fibreglass boat is stronger, less maintenance, you don't have to paint it every year, just wash it and anti-foul it. No like a wooden boat where you sand it down, prime it, undercoat it, gloss it every year and wear and tear on it. Fibreglass is a lot stronger. But a lot of people favour a wooden boat yet. It's more sea-kindly. There's nothing on it to stop the boat from rolling. The wooden boats, especially the clinker-built ones, are far more stable.

Mungo Montgomery

*Maritime Coastguard Agency

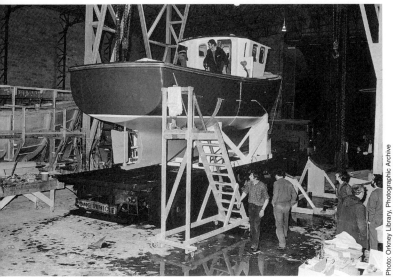

Photo: Orkney Library, Photographic Archive

fibre glass boat made by 'Halmatic', ready to be fitted out.

Westray Processors

WOMEN

For every job at sea, fishing, there are said to be ten ashore. Many of these jobs are done by women but traditionally women have not earned their living directly from the sea and, even now, it is still unusual. Many women ran the household and croft while their men were at sea. They were often engaged in baiting their husbands' fishing lines and mending their nets; hard, time-consuming work. They would meet the returning yoles. In Rackwick in Hoy, they waded waist-deep into the sea to haul the boats ashore. They then carried home the catch in heather creels on their backs; cleaned, split and dried the fish. Some Orkney women joined the many employed as gutters in the days of the herring fishing. Women still work in related industries, such as fish processing and preserving. The lifestyle associated with fishing and the Merchant Navy can mean that the job of keeping families and communities together falls to the women.

Photo: Orkney Library, Photographic Archive

Gutters, Stronsay

[While my father was at the herring] the land was worked by the womenfolk of the house, my mother and my grandmother and of course all us boys had to work round the house, singling turnips, gathering in the hay, even taking home the peats in the yole ...

Willie Groat, Longhope

They used to put them in a pot, there must have been water in the pot and they heated them, then it was easier to get the limpet out of the shell. ... it was mostly the women's job to knock them off the rocks, you used to have a pick or a hammer to knock them off, maybe a pailful. It was the men that were at sea but it was the women that got the bait for them.

When the men went to the herring, when they had the big boats, the women would bake and they took their supply of food with them for the week. Bannocks, they used to make bannocks.

Jenny Tulloch, North Ronaldsay

Very seldom that my mum ever left home because she was always doing ... she went to the kirk and things like that but if my dad caught fish she would be preparing and cleaning these fish; she had to milk the cows, make butter and cheese, all the washing to do for these children and

in those days on the farms you kept a pig, for the winter and she would prepare all that, stuff it up with oatmeal and onions and have meal puddings. She cooked and baked every single day of her life and she sewed and knitted all our clothes so she really didn't have much time to go away. It was one of these houses where people called every day and so there was all these cups of tea to be made as well, so there was always someone coming or going and so she had very little time.

Helen Manson, South Ronaldsay

Waiting for husbands, brothers and sons to return provides a source of real worry to families.

I used to worry. If I had a time for him to return and he didn't return on time. When he was away for a trip there is nothing I could do about it. My problem is ... if you can make a difference to their returning or not. So if they are due in at one and they don't come in ... and it's foggy, should you be starting to call the Coastguards at two or call the Coastguards at seven? Or not? How often can you do that? Do you do it this week and then need to do it three times from now on? ... It used to worry me and I used to do nothing.

Julie Gibson, Rousay

ISLAND LIVING

The mail arriving from Copinsay

ACCESS TO THE SEA

Everything that is not home-made or home-grown is brought to Orkney by boat. Everything that is sold outside the local community leaves by boat. This makes access to the sea important for any Orcadian community and particularly for those living in the North Isles.

Orcadian boats were designed to be light enough to haul up into a noust in the winter or rough weather but a pier or slip would give much easier access for bigger boats. For some communities, going to the kirk or the shop involved a trip by sea.

Meeting the steamer

A vehicle being ferried from the *M.V. Pole Star* to North Ronaldsay

Faray was all sea with small boats so I went out when I was between four and five years old, to go to the lobsters and go to Eday to do shopping. *Jock Harcus*

[We never went out on a Sunday] except to church. If it was a decent day we went over to Stronsay [from Papa Stronsay], the church was about two mile further up the isle, we used to walk to hid. *Jack Scott, Papa Stronsay*

[We] had to come over to Deerness, that was a half-hour trip in the motor boat and you had to walk up to the shop which was a mile, that was how we did it. We used to come over once a week, weather permitting. In winter weather you wouldn't get across in a fortnight … The yole came from Burray, built in St. Margaret's Hope … it was a good engine, it made a powerful difference. You could be sure of getting there but, with the tide against you and maybe the wind, you could sail back and forth, maybe two hours to get across and quite often in the winter it wasn't good weather either. You had to have your oilskins on … We were sometimes left in Deerness for two or three days before we could get back if it blew up.

Jimmy Groat, Copinsay

… the peat banks were above Melsetter and it was easier taking them home by sea than carting them home by the ox and cart. Sometimes we had to take some loads home by ox and cart but that meant leaving here about maybe four in the morning. The ox was very slow on the road, so we could take home a load of peats very easily in the boat because it was a light load. We would draw up against the westerly wind, beach the boat, let her ebb. Use a wheelbarrow to wheel all the peats down the hill. The peats were all in bags, heap them on board the boat and as the tide came in she would float off and we were allowed one mast. The yole had two masts but there wasno room to set the second … We'd drift down below a westerly wind down to Hackness here … My grandfather would come out to meet us and the ox and the cart. The ox would stand alongside the boat here and we would transfer the peats into the cart and then cart them home.

On one occasion I had forgotten to return the plug after draining the boat, I'd forgotten to put in the plug and the boat didn't seem to rise with the water when the tide came in and it struck me all of a sudden and I dived in like a terrier and here was a lovely spring bubbling up amongst the peats … My granny said that year 'Willie, the fire's out again … that's your salt water peats!'. *Willie Groat, Hoy*

The coal boat came once a year with coal for the lighthouse and that was how we got our coal, off that boat … It came on a big smack, it lay about half a mile out and they got the use of the coo boat for taking the coal into the pier,

then we had three horses and carts and we carted it at the expense of the coal boat and the lighthouse folk paid for that. We got paid for taking the coal up. One time they didn't have enough coal on the boat to pay him and they said they'd come back but they never. So the following year … father said 'I must get my coal first', so we got our pay first and carted the coal to the lighthouse and they were five ton short so they had to come back that year.

Jimmy Groat, Copinsay

Jimmy Groat remembers how complicated it was to move a family and a farm across the sea from Deerness to Copinsay.

The big coo boat was loaded up the day before and it was awful nice weather and we loaded up the coo boat with all the implements we could pack in it, all ready for the big day of flitting and then, on November 28th it was, we went down to the shore. It was dark in the morning and we had lanterns and the motor boat turned up and we got to Copinsay when it was more or less still dark and that gave us a good long day and we went back and forth all day with the coo boat and the animals and implements and all the folk came to watch, to enjoy the excitement of flitting … it was a great day. We finished about five o'clock and it was getting dark and father said 'Well it can blow if it likes now, we've flit', and it did blow then and no boat could get across for about a fortnight before we got back again. I think his tobacco was getting low by that time and he was anxious to get back.

This is flitting our stuff to Westray [from Papa Stronsay] when we moved they told us if we took the hen house over then it would save time. So that's me sitting on top of it. *Jack Scott*

Moving kye, Copinsay

We had no bother with them [the stock]. They just went aboard just as if they'd been doing it every day. We used a lot of straw as a decoy for them.

We made a ramp, made the side of the boat sloping so that the cattle would go up and get them in that way ... They never bothered ... The worst job was when we came back to Deerness, and the tide was in. Getting young animals off the boat, we just threw straw over the side on top of the water and they just walked over the side thinking it was alright and they more or less swam to the shore, nearly. They were glad to go ashore, they didn't stand in the sea.

You had to tie them in the boat in case they got a fright and tried to jump out.

Jack Scott remembers difficulties associated with shipping livestock across water from Stronsay to Papa Stronsay.

In our day the cattle had to be taken over in a flit boat. In fact, one time they used to swim them over. Once they got this flit boat cattle went in hid, horses was always swum. I remember one horse, they got him in the sea but twice he pulled the boat to the shore again. They blindfolded him and he walked all the way to Stronsay, just a wee bit in the middle where he had to swim and that's one I remember quite well ... It was quite a lot of hassle shipping animals for a small island.

There'd be very few coo boats around. I think that it was actually built for carrying barrels of herring ... It was a

sailing boat actually but it had to be towed and we towed it with a motor boat but it wasn't just built for sailing. It could sail if the wind was right but it wasnae the kind of boat you could just beat against the wind, it had a shallow draught and wide and no fast enough for sailing but they were alright if the wind was for'ard you sail around quite nicely.

One day, shipping a pig, they put a canvas over the hold to keep them in. They hadn't got very far when the pig's nose appeared under the canvas and next thing he was over the side and dad got the hind legs of it and I don't know how he got the strength to do it but he hauled it aboard ... he just gave a fearful heave and took him aboard ... John Fiddler was taking a ship out from Papay at the time and he saw it and he said 'Beuy, John, you just landed that like a cod'.

Uninhabited in recent years, Faray is still used by Westray farmers to graze sheep.

We started off with about two hundred yowes up to about nine hundred at one stage but now we are back down to seven hundred. The grass was overgrown when we first went there but now of course with all the sheep that's been eating so the grass comes back again so it's done weel ... we used to work with our own boat, a big wooden barge with a whole front that flapped doon, y'ken. It would take about eighty to a hundred lambs in that but that took us a long time to move maybe seven hundred lambs from Faray to Westray but now we get the *Eynhallow* ... they can lift out five hundred at a time so it doesn't take long ...

Marcus Hewison

Rowing across to the Holm of Grimbister, Firth

We used to do it all handled by hand and every bag [of fertiliser] was lifted seven times before it was getting ashore but now we do it with machinery and it's much easier ... Sheep'll no go in the sea unless they're pushed ... it doesna work. ... . They used to put them aff. There's a ring in the rocks doon their yet where they used to tie the bulls then they gied aft with a rope and a long rope and pulled them aff then they went underneath them with ropes and hoisted them on board a boat.

Marcus Hewison

Communities in the North Isles had particular problems if someone became sick or was injured, then medical help was only available on other islands or the Mainland.

We could use their [the herring boats] pier for our own use ... if it blew up we had to put the boat into a dock at the lower end of the island where there is a stage built of stone. Unfortunately it was tidal, you had to go down at half tide to get the boat out else you wouldn't get away ... when I was born they needed a doctor and they couldn't get the boat off because she was in the bottom so they had to take another boat from a neighbour's house, drag it over the beach, get it launched and went over to Stronsay for a doctor.

Jack Scott, Papa Stronsay

We was putting a patient to the hospital from Sanday. It was a bad night, there was a gale o'wind and I asked the doctor on Sanday if he'd come wi' us and he said he was coming in anyway because the man was very ill. We was coming up to the bay in Kirkwall I says to the doctor 'How was the patient?' and he says 'How long have we got?' and I says 'Ten minutes' and he says 'Well, he might make it'. They got him to hospital and that's the last I heard of him for maybe a year or so . Then I was in Stromness one time and we heard a bit of hilarity going on doon the pier and it was Shopping Week and we went to see what was going on and this was our old man standing on top o' a fish box, singing bothy ballads.

James Stout

Kirkwall Harbour

I broke my leg playing football, I was about thirteen, fourteen. I broke it on a Saturday night, lay in bed all day Sunday. Went into Kirkwall on the Monday, we reached Kirkwall about four. Went to hospital, got the leg set on Tuesday and back out on the Wednesday.

Harcus Scott, Westray

... you might get a call from the doctor to take a patient to the hospital, that happened several times until we got the plane service. I've seen us having to come direct from Westray with a hospital patient and then going and finishing our job after. That upset everything so when they got the plane it made all the difference.

John Burgher, Captain of the 'Earl Thorfinn'

During the war, carpenter Willie at Milldam was working with a circular saw and partly cut all his fingers off and they got in contact with the Corporal in charge [of the RAF lookout boat at Holland House] and he sent out a speedboat from Kirkwall ... they got him back into Kirkwall but they saved most of his fingers ...

John Cutt

For the smaller isles it has always been a challenge to survive in places with no ferry service and a limited pier. In many cases, islands have become uninhabited because it was no longer feasible to make a living where access to the sea was so difficult. Even today the building and locations of new pier and harbour facilities make for some of the liveliest debates amongst Orcadians, as they know businesses and livelihoods depend on good access to the sea. For the North Isles, a pier was essential to allow the steamers to visit and, in time, new piers were built to allow ro-ro ferries to operate as people became ever more reliant on motor transport.

Harbour Masters were employed by the local authority to oversee the harbour traffic. The shipping companies employed storemen to oversee the loading and off-loading of cargoes. Before the introduction of the ro-ro ferries, cars had to be hoisted on and off by crane. Animals were usually walked on board where possible but, for some of the smaller isles, they had to be placed in a sling then lifted on board by steam crane.

There was no roll-on roll-off so you had to arrange berthing for all the ships, all discharging on the pier and loading … the main problem was keeping the stuff on the pier moving because it was all coming off in bags or containers, stuff was stacked on the pier. In the spring you would have fertiliser from one end of the pier to another, you'd have cement coming, coal. Cargo going out, you had Highland Park whisky going out … a lot of cattle. You had the North of Scotland boats coming in about three or four times a week you see and they were all loading … you didn't have so many yachts came in then you see … The *St Rognvald*

was a regular trader … you could go on the *St Ninian* and you would leave Aberdeen, you could do a round trip from Aberdeen, Orkney, Shetland and then back to Aberdeen.

They all carried cattle, they were driven aboard. You had pens on the piers to keep the cattle in. They were all driven down the street to the mart, they were all sold in the mart then driven down onto the pier and they were loaded … half of them were mad, they would come ramping down the back road, down the pier, tearing all over the place, dockers chasing all over the place with sticks. That was quite true, it was like a rodeo.

William Sinclair, Harbour Master, Kirkwall

Looking after visiting boats and they all have harbour charges to pay and sometimes visiting fishing boats coming for whatever year, all you have to do is put into the Harbours Department weekly, their names, their departure times and where they are going. We have the weighbridge, that's me job as well.

Thomas B. Rendall, Harbour Master, Papa Westray

The *Hoy Head* unloading, Flotta

Photo: Chick Chalmers, Orkney Heritage

He was at the pier all the time, there was boats in with the discharging of the cargos, the loading of the cargos, the store at Kettletoft Pier. ... in my father's time it was the two steam ships.

It was mostly just labour. You were loading stock. The stock were all lifted on by crane or you had to go and lift it off. It was all barrel work after that and boxes and cartons of stuff etc., etc. It was all transported by barrel in the early days then we moved on to palleted cargo.

There was no communication at all. You could watch, you had eyes and you could see. You could tell where the ship was going to go next. If she was coming from Sanday to Eday or something you could see her coming. If she skipped Sanday and went to Stronsay you could rest assure that something was wrong and you could get a telephone connection to Stronsay when she arrived there and find out why. But before that there was no telephone.

There was always problems. It couldn't be any other way when you had a lot of loose cargo going from island to island. There must be something going out to a wrong island and disappearing.

We lost cattle and everything down the side of the boat. You've got to salvage it the best you could. I've seen cattle between the ship and the quay. You've got to ease the ship off, give it room to struggle then maybe you'd get a rope around it. Of course they go out to sea as well ... they go away from the shore and out to sea ... in the early days all the cattle were used to being roped and tied and led. As farming got more commercial that was when we had the problem because the cattle were led down the pier like a dog on a lead ... the problem was when the loose cattle came down the pier, nothing to hold them in, nothing between the sides of the pier and the sea and them milling around, they push one another over the pier ... then they got the penning arrangements.

They used to do that before they came, ballast the tanks so that she had a bit of list to work the cargo, then made her shipshape before they went to sea again.

Then there was stock days; going out on a Monday, stock went out on Thursdays then, the busy time of the year at the back end of the year, when they wanted to get rid of their stock, there were extra shipping put on to get rid of their stock. They were deposited in pens at the end of the pier and they had all got to be loaded by hand and that was a very difficult situation. That pen had stood there for maybe an hour and a half before the boat came and just imagine trying to get that lot loaded up a gangplank depending on what the sea might allow you and it was very difficult. I've seen them leave here with seventy or a hundred on a special shipping day.

Very difficult for the audience that was watching. Very difficult for you loading. Very difficult for the stock. Sometimes you could move them very easy if they had a notion that's way they were going to go they would go but other times it would be difficult to get them started to go but once they started they would go, you could get them loaded.
Jimmy Wilson, Sanday Shipping Agent

Pilots guided vessels from elsewhere through particularly difficult pieces of water, such as the Pentland Firth or Scapa Flow or into harbours, assisting them to berth.

My grandfather was a patriarch. He had a big beard way down, covering his chest ... he did the pilotage of the ships coming in here and we would go off in the *Daisy* to meet a ship that was slowing down and all we got was a rope from the flying bridge that was dropped down to us. If we were nimble enough we caught hold of it. My father would go up that rope then, hand over hand and every now and then he would pull his beard to one side because it was getting mixed up with his hands and he could climb on board. There were two coal hulks in the bay here and these ships came in from the Baltic and came in to get more coal before going west to America. It was always a head wind to get to America. My grandfather would take ashore telegrams to the owners to tell them where they were and they would be able to deal with that at the local post office. It saved the men from having to launch a boat and they would leave my father with instruction of what they wanted in the way of lamb, vegetables etc., dairy produce; cheese, butter, eggs ... and my father would slaughter the lamb and have it dressed and carried off to the boat the next day ... there was no cash transactions. It was always bartered for something else, perhaps a short length of manila rope and we had a rope-making machine and we could make the rope the size we wanted. These were great hawsers and we'd strand them down and make our own ropes and cover them with beeswax, make them the size we needed. Other things such as Fray Bentos corned beef, big six pound tins of it ... They were cargo ships.

It would be May before you'd see the first boats arriving here ... On one occasion they had been in here for their bunkers to go back home and it was a fair wind and the old *Daisy* couldn't catch this sailing ship when it was under sail and just sort of signaled that they were carrying on, they werenae going to turn back ... So they just took my grandfather along with them and he spent the winter over in Sweden ... They said they would come back with him in springtime.
Willie Groat, Longhope

'Over carrying' still happens occasionally if a ship is keen to get away and cannot stop to let the pilot disembark.

My husband acted as pilot for the ships coming in. It started in the springtime, in March when the big spring tides are and the big salt ships from Spain with a cargo of salt for curing and it was stored here. *Meg Fiddler*

There were two men that worked at piloting in the village. That was like when the stock boats, the bigger boats coming in they would go off take them in … there was such competition between these two men, piloting the boats. They were going great distances to pick up the boats and these were the boys who we were watching them come in … *James Work*

William Sinclair worked as Harbour Master in Kirkwall and as a pilot, first independently, then after 1970 for Orkney Harbours.

They would call you up on the radio and say they needed a pilot for coming into Kirkwall harbour. The Assistant Harbour Master usually took the boat out and I went aboard and then he went ahead of us and berthed, took the ropes and moored the ship up. The local ones didn't bother with pilots it was just strangers, timber boats or grain or tankers, they would take pilots. I just worked on my own then …

It was all types. The Captain of the ship was still in charge but then you advised him or he might just say 'you go and berth the ship'. It really depended on how he felt.

A lot of them [foreign ships] were Norwegian or Danish and they all spoke very good English. A sight better than we could speak their language I'm afraid.

I did the North Isles. Maybe a ship would come into Kirkwall with fertiliser, maybe going to Westray or maybe Stronsay …

The oil tankers, which are now such a common sight in Scapa Flow, presented a new challenge for local pilots.

I had never been piloting these size of ships in my life but there was two or three pilots who came here who had done it so what we did, maybe two, three pilots go together, there was two or three chaps who came here who had been out in the Far East in Saudi Arabia and they had handled these kind of ships before, you know and they showed us how to do it properly and after a while you got a licence.

They are just big tankers, they are roughly about a thousand feet long, usually and about seventy-, or eighty- or maybe ninety-thousand ton, that's the kind of breed that comes here … They are very slow, sluggish … and take a long time to stop and go astern … they take a lot of wind too, because they are high so they can drift … they are a different thing altogether, there is no comparison with small boats.

Now there are compulsory pilotage areas around Orkney and the local Harbour Authority employs nine pilots to guide ships through these areas. All the piers and harbours in Orkney were taken-over by the Harbour Authority in 1977. St Margaret's Hope is the only remaining Trust port. Since the inception of the Flotta Oil Terminal, the Harbour Authority also has three tugs which assist oil tankers berthing in Scapa Flow

The tugs are used to berth the big tankers in Scapa Flow. You have them on the towers to hold them steady because you can't do much with them, it's just like a big box, floating from side to side so if you are going onto the jetty you have to have the tugs to hold them on or off the jetty … you had a radio and you would speak to the tugs the whole time … it didn't do your heart any good, sometimes in the wintertime when you'd see the jetty come rushing at you … They are just there to carry oil, there's no beauty. *William Sinclair*

ORKNEY AND THE SEA

Tanker at Flotta

Photo: Orkney Library, Photographic Archive

Hoy Head

FERRIES

The ferry services in Orkney have provided the lifeblood of the islands, taking people and freight where they need to go. Regular steamer services began in the North Isles in the 1860s, and in the South Isles in the 1890s. The North Isles had a weekly, or in North Ronaldsay's case, fortnightly service. Most people had no need to travel beyond their own island more than occasionally. Schoolchildren stayed in the hostel in Kirkwall for a whole term at a time from the age of eleven. Daily services now allow people to commute to work on different islands and the air services allow most of the isles daily contact with the mainland taking care of the mail, the newspapers and emergency medical cases. Schoolchildren can now go home to the isles every weekend.

North Ronaldsay trip day

Photo: Orkney Library, Photographic Archive

It was a big event [when the steamer came] because it was so seldom … everybody went down … a lot of people went down just to help them and then up to the post office to wait for the mail. In the wintertime especially because there was no other excitement … You didn't go to Kirkwall unless you had to … School kids was the biggest out-going and in-going passengers I suppose. There was a yearly trip day to Kirkwall … and everybody went on that, just for the day, but it was nearly seven hours in the sea with the old boats.

Oliver Scott, North Ronaldsay

She [the *Earl Sigurd*] did North Ronaldsay. Many times she had to stand by most of the week to get it done.

John Burgher, Captain of the Thorfinn

The steamer was only once a fortnight, weather permitting but the mail boat three times a week … it took a whole day sometimes to get into Kirkwall. You had to cross to Sanday, then you had to get across Sanday. You had to walk or hire a car then get into the steamer, the *Earl Sigurd* or the *Earl Thorfinn* and if it went past Westray, it took a whole day, nearly.

Jenny Tulloch, North Ronaldsay

Delayed? It was never on time. I've seen it two hours late. Just imagine you leave Kirkwall to go to Westray. You start out at Kirkwall maybe six thirty in the morning then you went to Eday first, it varied, Stronsay, Sanday, Papa Westray then Westray. You'd be in to Westray late in the day, it was a long day aboard.

Jimmy Wilson

There werna a lot of passengers in that day .... You couldn't do a day return. Otherwise you would go in on Monday and not get back until Wednesday.

How long did it take to get to Kirkwall from Westray?

It seemed to be for ever … I'd years of it. The six years I was at Stromness school and the four years I was in Edinburgh. We leave here at seven o'clock in the morning and quite frequently it would be three o'clock in the afternoon when you got there … You were just aboard for the day. The first thing you did when you got aboard was order your breakfast and order your dinner and you just settled down for a day on the sea .... It was quite usual to spend a couple of hours in Stronsay and a couple of hours in Sanday … we used to get off and wander about … you used just go up the pier and walk about. After a bit you got to ken folk and you'd have a bit of a yarn. Different way of life.

Harcus Scott, Westray

Working on a ferry offered a regular living at sea, returning home more often than if you were fishing. Wages were poorer but the work was steady. You started as an Ordinary Seaman, progressing to Able Seaman after three years sea-time and then, if you wanted to go for your ticket, it was possible to become a Mate or Skipper. Alex Costie worked from Westray as a deck-hand. John Burgher worked his way up to Captain of the 'Earl Thorfinn' and Jock Harcus was an Engineer on the 'Earl Thorfinn' and the 'Earl Sigurd'.

It was long hours and hard work on that boat … people kept hundreds of hens out in the isles so you had all the feeding for that and cattle feed and slag and cement and gas bottles. Boxes coming down late at night marked perishable and they were maybe full of barbed wire or something and then on the way back in it was eggs and cattle and sheep and horses. Everything that was needed had to be carted back and fore. I thought it was very poor pay we got at that time. You had to put in eight hours as a seaman and eight hours as a docker before you got any overtime … I can never understand why I stayed there so long. … I got married about that time … and I was looking for a suitable job I suppose.   *Alex Costie*

You wereny home on Monday or Tuesday, at home on Wednesday night, then you were away on Thursday and Friday night, home on Saturday night and Sunday

John Burgher

We came home every night, more or less, but it did have sleeping accommodation if need be. Just bunk beds. You took your own grub with you when I joined first, you just had a wee case with your own grub. The Captain, Engineer and the Mate they got their grub but the crew didn't. It was just the way of Orkney Steam. We were lucky if we got a week off but we just accepted that, it was your job.

Jock Harcus

A typical day would be Kirkwall to Eday and then to Stronsay, then to Sanday then up to Westray. It was a long day and you had to keep the cargo separate for each of that islands and sometimes you would stop up in Calf Sound as well. If you had done Eday in the morning, you might get a commercial traveller going ashore there and he would go around the merchants in Eday and the boat would pick him again from a boat in Calf Sound.

The cooking facilities were just not great. How we managed to cook on it I just do not know. They never knew how many people they were going to be having for meals either you see. Everybody wanted to have their meal while the boat was in at the pier. They didna want to eat when they were rolling about.

If a passenger had a lot of suitcases you could put them among the cargo. You just marked them with a tally on it saying 'with passenger'. There was one time we were at Egilsay and an old fella came on board with a coo and a tally round its lug saying 'with passenger' … he wasna wanting to pay freight on it … I thought we must be giving him a free passage for that.

You were quite often having to discharge the cargo in an awful panic because the harbours weren't so good and they were shallow and you were trying to get the cargo out before the boat got stuck on the bottom. You had to get away when the tide was right.

I had the cold for nearly all the time I was there. You were sweating working away putting out the cargo and sometimes you are working by the steam pipes in the hold, very warm and then you'd go down underneath where the capstan was, it was a very draughty, cold, horrible place. I seemed to have the cold the whole time.   *Alex Costie*

Alex Costie

Rescuing a cow, Sanday

It was all there, what we needed. There was nothing posh about it.   *Jock Harcus*

We had a wireless for a wee while ... see you know in that days you had the accumulator and the dry battery and in that pitch o' sea it would knock the whole thing down ... there werenae very much to do apart from read the paper but sometimes you were that tired you were just thankful to go to bed and sleep. It was a lot o' hard work ... you cooked for yourselves. No cooking for the crew in that days. You might take a wee dish o' stew and, if you got delayed, the next thing you knew the whole thing was burnt.

Miserable. Way down the fore end, there were eight of us down there ... you had to shove them some place that wasn't suitable for cargo. Steel box ... if your bare skin came in contact with that on a cold, frosty night it wasn't very nice. We used to have board between us and the steel box. They didn't care much for the comfort of the crew at that time.

In the *Earl Thorfinn* you could go down the engine room. If you were on good terms with the Engineer well, there was a bucket with warm water. You couldn't splash it about the engine or you would never get in there again.

We just walked them [livestock] on board. Sometimes you had to sling them if the tide was bad, special slings ... In the first of me days we were carrying horses as well, before they got onto tractors ... It cooled them off. If you had some awkward ones, by the time they got ashore they werenae awkward.   *John Burgher*

We got radar which was a great help with the fog. We had our times to go and if you couldna see it wasna easy but

the Captain was good at that. It was all well timed, you knew exactly that if you were leaving Kirkwall, twenty-two and a half minutes later you were at Shapinsay at the west side, there was no other place that you could be, they just worked on that system ...   *Jock Harcus*

If you got a heavy rain storm, many a time it would be like looking into a bowl of muck. Snow wasn't bad but I've seen rain just about blotting the whole thing out.

Unloading the *Hoy Head*, 1974

Sometimes I enjoyed it, sometimes I got sick fed up o' it. No matter what happens, the skipper got the blame. It was a job to please them all but we got on with it no bad.

John Burgher

We carried every kind of agricultural thing that we could; cattle, sheep, pigs, horses, binders everything like that.

They got it on with a crane, steam winch. Everything had to be handled separately. I had my training in the Flow, and it was just the same kinda thing on the *Sigurd*.

When I was there in the morning I was usually there an hour and a quarter before sailing time just checking to see that everything was OK. No water dripping anywhere or steam hissing. At that time there was no other noise about and you could easy pinpoint anything and then we usually opened the fire doors and get steam up then you did your usual like heating up the engine by putting steam through it. It usually took about ten minutes

When the ship was sailing I was just seeing that everything was going right and feeling the bearings checking that they werna getting hot, putting a drop of oil on, and you had to see if the steam was keeping up right and putting more coal on.

The safety aspects were up to yourself. I had to watch the ones that was working with me, firemen, they would do anything daft and check them on it right away, we had to learn them to look after themselves.

Jock Harcus

The South Isles were served by a number of different boats including the 'Hoy Head' and the 'Ailsa' and, prior to the the building of the Barriers, the 'St Ola' stopped at St Margaret's Hope to take on mail.

The steam *Hoy Head* was built to be a tug, she was a tuggy shape, it was a good old boat though. There was an Engineer on it two hours from Stromness and he had been a deep sea engineer and he said that the engines on the *Hoy Head* were working like a clock. He kept them in that good order.

The *Hoy Head* was all local knowledge, Donald Sinclair he kent everybody and if you wanted anything teen from Stromness, just tell him and he would get it for you doon at night. Local knowledge is great thing. They were very reliable men. If you wanted a bottle of whisky just tell them

Jock Harcus

usay Post Boat

Photo: Orkney Library, Photographic Archive

and they would take it to you, we all had a bottle of whisky for Christmas and New Year and that was the way that you got it. There was no pub on Flotta so you just telt that men to take it down and you gave them the money.

The only training that that men got was just their own fishing experience ...   *Malcolm Ross*

There have been four 'St Ola's' taking passengers across the Pentland Firth; the first in 1892. At one time the crews were exclusively Orcadian,

The *Earl Sigurd*

Photo: Orkney Library, Photographic Archive

working throughout the busy season. Walter Leask served from 1949 until 1983 as Purser on three of the 'St Olas'.

We stayed in Graham Place and the old *Ola*, the steam *Ola*, used to reverse, come astern right to below my window, at quarter past eight in the morning so that was my alarm for going to school at nine o'clock. I could see her through my window and she had a big triple expansion with a big prop' and she went thrum thrum and I'd think 'Rising time again' ... I didn't realise that I was going to be on her.

Before [the ro-ro service] you had to lift each car individually and plenty of people would go away from here in the morning and they would maybe only get their car at four in the afternoon.

I've seen me doing double runs with just one ship, working until three in the morning and then starting again at seven. The cars would be queuing up, there was no bookings.

The Mate and you went round to collect the tickets. We could only take about three cars and that was if the tide was right. If the tide was too low then we couldn't get clearance at Scrabster to lift them on the Pier. She was a bit like a glorified trawler ... she was a good able ship, she had to be, to do the Firth for fifty-eight years ... we had big crates of livestock, a hook in each corner and then there was horseboxes ... the livestock shared with the steerage passengers.

You limited the amount of passengers to the livestock you had.

The 'St Ola' (1951 – 1974) could carry six vehicles but unloading could take some time.

They never could really cut the time much in the Firth because in thirty miles ten minutes was a big difference. I don't suppose there was ten minutes of difference between the diesel and the old steam *Ola*, but the steam *Ola* could go into the inner berth when the diesel ship couldn't for she could bring up in a shorter distance with the amount of power she had in the big prop', whereas the diesel was twins and took longer to bring up. So very often we were lined up for getting into the pier and the Harbour Master would flash 'Don't try it'. I would be very unpopular. I had to go round the passengers and tell them we were on our way back and oh, the moans! It was usually a bad day when we couldn't get in and I had to tell them they had it to do all over again.

When we saw this big ship coming, the ro-ro we said 'Oh boy that one will be alongside the pier a lot'. But the reverse was true because of the fact of the bigger pier acted as a breakwater. The first year of the ro-ro there was maybe two days we didn't sail.

In the early days of the ro-ro there was maybe a day and a half you couldn't sail and it was always the berth that was the reason … it would be most unusual if it was the weather alone. She can take a heck of a thumping. As we did many a time.

The second *Ola* was from 1951 to 1974 all that time we handled all the butter and cheese and stuff from the creamery, came across and was loaded onto lorries in Scrabster so very often vehicles were left at the back of this stuff and the poor passengers had to wait until all this had been manhandled on board, you know ten ton of butter or cheese and very often it was three or four o'clock in the afternoon before they got away … It was always people who had small cars who could go down in the lower hold. In fact we even put cars down there that were longer than the hatch by putting a short strop on one side and hanging them at an angle … It was amazing how little damage was done with the cars. The boys handled them very well. Very occasionally a rear light went or something but it wasn't very often.

I enjoyed meeting people. I made a lot of friends, you know, a lot of people came annually. You saw the same old faces. Some said 'It's not the same now Walter, we don't see your face at Scrabster and ken we're nearly home'. I became part of the works with being there nearly thirty-four years.

The 'St Ola III' (1974 – 1992) earned the nickname the 'Roly-poly Ola'.

She was a grand sea boat but, oh, she liked to roll. We always said she would roll on wet grass. She did it without any excuse at all. Much to the annoyance of the passengers. And yes, she flung quite a few people … We had one poor girl, she shot across in front of my office window and she hit the window and she broke her wrist on the handrail … She ran out on the deck and I said we would take her into my office but she said 'I'm no shifting' and she wouldn't shift off the deck. I sent the stewards to tell the Captain, to see if there was anyone on board who could help … There turned out to be a Norwegian doctor on board … and he put her hand in splints … Her auntie was sitting alongside her and … she shot off and went burling around as if she was on a gramophone, skrekking too. It was a right day for them …

There was an officers' union and a seaman's union. There was about six weeks and there was a strike on board and we had to go down every morning at eight o'clock and come off at four in case the strike went off because we weren't on strike, it was the seamen … We scrubbed oot cabins, we painted deck heads. There is nothing more monotonous than a ship lying alongside, no even with her engine going.

Latterly they went to this week-on and week-off business and I couldn't believe the difference and I got leave in the middle of the summer. I went fishing and I kept expecting to hear someone shout from the shore 'Oi, get back to your work!'.

There have been a number of other boats which have taken passengers across the Firth. In 1971 the 'Pentland Atom' started crossing the Pentland Firth, described once as the smallest thing that could cross the Firth that wasn't a seagull. The 'Pentalina' crossed from 1972 until 1974 from John o'Groats to St Margaret's Hope then the 'Atom' was changed to the 'Pentland Spray' and went from Burwick to John o'Groats until 1976 when the boat was changed to the 'Pentland Venture', a purpose built vessel. Now the 'Pentalina B' offers a ro-ro service from St Margaret's Hope to a specially constructed pier at Gill's Bay. All of these boats have been initiated and operated by local people (from Orkney or Caithness).

There have always been ways of getting across the water if the ferry wasn't convenient. It used to be possible to travel to Sanday from North Ronaldsay with the mail boat or to hire a private

Rousay Post Boat

boat to get you across the Firth. It was possible to earn a little extra income by providing a one-off or regular service if there was any demand.

That's the boat that's done the school run since 1967, until the *Marianna* arrived … it's really like a taxi service on the sea, you just have folk phoning up when they want to go across the sea … the start of this was a teacher moving into Papay and needing a job. It was decided to take the secondary school passengers into Westray each day and she came with us for twenty year.   *Thomas B. Rendall, Westray*

I mind a funeral, the weather had been bad and the *Islander* couldn't get the remains of a certain person into Papay. They could get into Pierowall but not into Papay, so I was hired to do the job. They had been delayed for about a week and they were kinda anxious … it was OK for a smaller boat. It didna happen very often, but sometimes you got a bad week in winter.   *Edwin Groat, Papa Westray*

We just ran among the islands. We just did anything, worked it along wi' the lobster fishing … you could leave Kirkwall and get a taxi to Carness and a boat from Carness to Shapinsay and a taxi to the Ness of Shapinsay

and we would pick you up from Shapinsay and take you to Stronsay. That was roughly in the same time that the ferry boat can do it yet. Cars wereny so popular and we just landed you below the house, if you wanted, wi a small boat … A hire to Kirkwall was two pound.

Jimmy Stout, Stronsay

North Ronaldsay people who went into Kirkwall on the post boat to Sanday had to negotiate Black Rock at Otterswick in Sanday. Depending on the tide they either faced a scrabble down rocks or a lift from the boatman.

Black Rock [Sanday] there was no jetty there, it was, just to go down and sometimes the boatman just had to carry folk on his back … it was quite an experience.

Jenny Tulloch, North Ronaldsay

I had some horrible crossings, very sick in those days. It was better going away. Coming home you could be stuck in Sanday for days.   *Oliver Scott, North Ronaldsay*

St Ola II going through Hoy Sound, 1950s

[The mail boat] could take a football team and hangers-on. We used to play football against Sanday . . . the boat from Kirkwall only came once a fortnight so that was our main transport, I suppose. We used to get the mail boat to Sanday, cross Sanday to Kettletoft then the boat to Kirkwall . . . it took about four hours if you were lucky but it could take the whole day.   *Oliver Scott, North Ronaldsay*

I took a lot of people across the Firth . . . it was great outings many a time . . . we went across a lot, shipping lobsters . . . sometimes we were across there and there were people wanting to come back . . .

Willie Mowatt, South Ronaldsay

I mind Jimmy Shand came to Stronsay once and we crossed fae Stronsay to Eday sixteen times in one night. Just run the whole night.   *Jimmy Stout*

Captain John Burgher and the crew of the *Earl Thorfinn*

Landing place, Wyre

Ro-ro ferry *Eynhallow*, Tingwall

Photo: Kate Towsey

Ro-ro ferry *Eynhallow*, Tingwall

Photo: Kate Towsey

The Royal Bank of Scotland's floating bank, *Otter Bank* at the slip beside the Shapinsay pier, mid 1960s. Manager John Beavan and a customer

THE OTTER BANK

The ferries were not the only boats regularly servicing the North Isles. There had been shop boats which serviced the isles up until the Second World War but in the 1960s the National Commercial Bank, later the Royal Bank of Scotland, thought it was worth their while to send a mobile branch to the North Isles through the summer months. There were no ro-ro services so that meant fitting out a boat as a bank. The 'Otter Bank' travelled around the North Isles from 1962 to 1970, meeting customers at the pier, on a timetable dictated by the tides and the weather and with working hours few other bank officials kept.

Willie Groat worked as the bank official and David Irving skippered the boat with a number of assistants helping through the summer. During the rest of the year Willie travelled to the North Isles on the ferry, meeting customers in local premises near the pier.

I was the accountant in Kirkwall, I was the most easily spared and I went out to the isles, to Stronsay and Westray to try and develop the connection after the war and once a month was too seldom. I went out there with ferry boat and went all round the isles, started off about quarter past six and finished up at Westray about quarter past five and then start work and we'd go on to midnight. You were lucky if you got anything to eat in that time …

Going to North Ronaldsay the boat would leave at something like quarter to six … I would go down the night before and I would haul out some of the life-jackets and put the cash in there and [during the journey] I would sleep up against there with my head but I would have another 'cash' bag which contained outdoor clothes.

I would go back to the hotel [after work] where I had a bed for the night. Sometimes it wasn't worth ruffling up the bed, I'd just lie on top of it because you'd be leaving at six o'clock in the morning … Then Stronsay, it was just as bad, until midnight … I came back and I said 'Why don't we develop our own boat?' … I knew the *Otter* very well because it

belonged to my cousin … this was kept very hush-hush in fact our communication with head office was in code.

We were out five days a week. On Monday morning we went out to Egilsay, Wyre, Rousay. That was a day's work and back in. Tuesday we went to Shapinsay and Eday, that was another day's work. Wednesday morning we set off very early to Papa Westray. We'd arrive at Papa Westray when the school was coming out at lunch-time and all the children came down to play on the top deck … it was a sort of popular place … then we went over to Westray, we still had a sub-office at Westray. We opened the office at three o'clock and again we were open until midnight. Thursday morning we went down to Westray all the way down to Stronsay and back again. Sometimes we stayed and went over to Sanday for the Friday. So it was nine islands in a week. Saturday, I went into the office to get more cash, get all my ledgers cleared. If I had any transactions with other banks I'd go round and see them and 'your customer came in and asked for ten pounds out of his account and he signed this receipt' … we looked after their customers for them. It was a standing agreement among the banks.

M.V. *Otter Bank* at Wyre pier

Being able to travel to all of the North Isles and have time to serve the customers took careful calculation of tides and conditions.

We couldn't leave Rousay out but we'd take an extra man out to Westray and we'd leave him to get the main steamer down to Stronsay and he would hold the fort there for the day. We would leave very early from Westray and we'd lean the boat against the pier so we got extra fuel on the weather-side, that depended on the wind of course. That meant we had more ballast on the windward side and we'd set off then to North Ronaldsay. That was below the horizon and we'd take a turn of two hours on and two hours off and we'd sleep in between times. The tide was with us. When we got to North Ronaldsay it was still flowing water and folks could come on board. We'd get the last of the flood tide which would take us round Sanday, still the tide on the stern and it would draw us up to Stronsay

and we would pick up our man there, he would be waiting on the pier for us … with the cash bag of course and out through out the west opening and away home. We would cross to the Green Holms and when we got there the flood was just starting and it would push us right home. From early morning to when we got home the tide was on our stern. We had to work this out, otherwise we couldn't have managed it.

We were never slovenly dressed. Davey and I were properly dressed behind the counter and I think that's important – image. We weren't there on holiday.

The harbour in Kirkwall was our front door and the Galt at Shapinsay was our front gate. Most days we'd go down to the front door and go down to the Galt in Shapinsay and look at it there and say 'Well it's not worth going home now, we might as well go on' … We were quite adept at handling the boat. We knew the North Isles like the back of our hands.

M.V. Otter Bank at Egilsay pier

L-R: Alice Flaws of Ha'brake, Wyre, Willie Groat, Neil Flaws of Ha'brake, at the Wyre pier
to visit the National Commercial Bank's *Otter Bank*. David Irvine is in the wheelhouse.

*There were, of course, some compensations for
the long hours worked in the service of the bank.*

On the Calf of Eday, Davey Irving, my skipper, liked gulls'
eggs and I would have an extra man on board and he
would go ashore with Davey onto the Calf of Eday and they
would spend maybe half an hour gathering eggs and Davey
would have two black back's eggs for his breakfast. He had
a constitution like a horse.

We fished our own fish as we went along and we set our
own creels and we had our own crab and lobster … when
we knew the places to fish and we just wanted a nice size
for the pan, not too big and if they were bigger we cleaned
them and dried and took them home with us … if the fish
didn't flap its tail in the pan then it wasn't just quite fresh.

Willie Groat

NAVENA

SEA CONDITIONS

Learning about tides, navigation skills and being able to predict weather conditions were essential to staying alive. Only experience could teach fishermen how to read the weather and local sea conditions, to predict bad weather approaching and to know when to run for home. Still, every year fishermen are lost at sea despite modern technology.

They were very careful about the weather. The barometer was tapped religiously. If there was any doubt about it you would refrain from going. It wasn't worth the risk. It was bad enough being out in an open boat.

It was explained to us very carefully, there was certain dangerous areas, such the beacon below Cantick. The tide runs very strongly there. A wave can come up unexpectedly there and sweep you away from there. I have never been to the Beacon in my life because we were told it was unsafe. Certain rocks too … we never ventured where it was unsafe.   *Willie Groat, Longhope*

Each main tide had a set up because of its power, it coils back … so it takes quite a while to learn them all … one or two of them can be very dangerous … they can come on … rapidly if there's a head wind … There's only certain bits of the island you can land … on the rocky side then … you have to be careful there.

I think we learnt all the tidal sets in the first two or three years. And then of course when the tides start or finish there's a set time I mean calendar times or moon times … it's easy to judge them … but when you come out to the deep water the high water on the land will run out there for maybe two or three miles off … maybe for another two or three hours … this is something you must consider if going distance fishing for like mackerel or haddock … you've got to consider that or know that.

It also had to be fairly accurate when you were fishing in deep water because the creels were taken down by strong tide. You had to be out there when the tide was slack, it might only be half an hour or an hour at the most and the next tide will come in.   *Willie Muir, North Ronaldsay*

Swell is different from ordinary chop. It is caused by a gale some distance away, maybe the tops of the swell is two hundred to three hundred feet apart and coming in long slow rollers. Sometimes they'd break on the top but in certain conditions they were very liable to upset a narrow boat that was trying to cross the swell. Particularly if it broke at the top of the swell. You could get very confused water there.   *Cyril Annal, South Ronaldsay*

Jock o'Bloomfield told me a story about leaving Shetland in blind fog and the first piece of land they seen was out at the Ness in Burray. That was just under sail with a compass and a watch. Their navigation was spot on.

Mungo Montgomery, Burray

I can remember a boat coming from Fair Isle with haddocks and he sold them for three shillings a score. It came down thick fog but it didn't bother them, off they went. They wouldn't be many lengths from the pier before they disappeared.   *John Cutt, North Ronaldsay*

Before we got the radar you couldn't see what you were doing, you were just going blind. You would run your course and you would run your time that it took to get from one point to another but you couldn't guarantee you would strike that point … Going through Calf Sound there's a big Head on each side. We used to come in through there with a whistle. You would blow the whistle and if you were right in the middle you would get both echoes coming in at the same time and you knew then you were right in the centre … some would take more risk than what others would do. I mind one time we came down there. It was a bonny day but there was an awful fog hanging about the Heids and the skipper that was on, he was very good at the fog, too, he couldna get the signals so that he knew he was safe. Some boy that was at the wheel said if someone would go up the mast we might see the Heid through it. Of course I was the youngest and up the mast I had to go and right enough I could see the Red Heid coming through the fog. So I said it to them and pointed out where it was and they said 'are you sure that's the Red Heid?' and I looked the other side and said 'There is the Grey Heid on the other side'. 'Oh, that's alright.' We came in through that and we had no more fog that day. Why he trusted me I don't know. It worked.

John Burgher, Westray

I think now people are losing their natural ability to go back. When I was first with Roberston's I was with old Sandy Sutherland, he used to in his days away with Roberston's and any time I was home I used to have a long yarn with him down the pier and he would say 'Boy, in me days there was no radars, open bridge' and I said 'How did you navigate Sandy?' and he said 'With the greatest of ease: skill'. If it was fog they had a Norwegian foghorn, an old thing that you wound up and it would let off a blast and they could time the blast, the time it took leaving the ship and the time it took the echo to come back and by that they could work out roughly where they were off. That, to me, is real seamanship … I always think when it's a bad night I go back to basics of taking a bearing and distance then checking it up with all this aids to navigation.

Willie Tulloch, Stromness

Rousay Post Boat in a gale

Cloud conditions. Look at the cloud conditions. Look at the swell over the previous number of days … a long number of days and you could predict the gales by the amount of swell that was in the sea. Changes in the tide … The one thing above all is keep watching the horizon and if the conditions changed on the horizon suddenly. It was time to make for home … I do all those things that those guys did and then I go in and listen to the weather forecast.

… you can get a local gale that's unexpected. If you keep your eyes open you can see bad weather coming and that it's time to get home.   *Cyril Annal*

I was going to put the fish on board the *St Ola*, I was going to put the fish on the *Ola* on the Friday because I just didn't want to bother going over … and the Captain came down 'Alfie what are you putting that fish on board for?' and I said 'I wasn't feeling like going over today'. And he said 'What? I don't think we'll make it today'. So I said 'I'd better take the fish back on board' and I took the

Rosemary's fish the same day and I said to the Harbour Master 'Give them a ring in Scrabster and tell them I might be about an hour late but I'm heading across', to keep the buyers there. We set off and the *Ola* came down to off Aurora Head and they took a roll, the lifeboats touched the water and the *Ola* turned to come back to Stromness and we carried on and landed and when we came back that night we had a whole dose of passengers. We had the minister, the doctor's wife … it was in the wintertime and it was pitch dark, six, seven o'clock at night … They were all stuck up in the wheelhouse with me and we ran into a lump of water, just a wall of water and it took all the ropes back against the wheelhouse, the whole damn lot and it knocked the wheelhouse windows in. I had a big thick jersey on and I tell you one thing it was some cold but I got the wheelhouse to myself after that. It would never have happened if I could have got across to ease the engine down … there was too many people in there … the fish we had on board, we had to get them landed because our wages depended on it.   *Alfie Sinclair, Stromness*

Captain John Burgher here tells the story of the memorable night in 1953 when the 'Earl Thorfinn' was caught by bad weather and was blown to Aberdeen.

We were going out on the Saturday to go around the islands again, finish up on Westray but we never got to an island, the storm came on us. We could see nothing, just a proper blizzard, so we were blown afore the storm … [we ended up in] Aberdeen. A northerly wind you see, it was blowing on her stern, she wouldnae keep her heid to the wind. She was just helpless … We had about a dozen passengers from various pieces. One old man had been to Dundee, he came across the pier to go to Sanday and ended up in Aberdeen. I was a deck-hand [at the time] … Steam steering gear, hid broke doon, it was a good job otherwise it would probably smashed the whole thing. We had to steer her with the hand gear, but we werenae fit to pull her ower. And we were right tired by the time we got doon to Aberdeen … We was down there about ten o'clock at night … We were just trying to keep her steering afore the wind if she had gone broadside onto it she would have likely turned right ower … there was some awful lumps o' weather.

I don't think it was forecast but the barometer was terribly low … It's just lucky we wereny all drowned. It was more than the ship was game for … [The passengers] were just hanging on below … there was no contact [with the shore] at all, nobody knew where we were … We hoped we had an idea of where we might be, you just had no idea how she was being driven. The first light we seen was Kinnaird, that's about Fraserburgh … It's a single flash. It took a bit of convincing to make sure it was Kinnaird, it might have been a ship for all we ken, but the weather was eased a bit by then but there was a terrible sea running … We had to make sure then that we weren't going to strike Rattray, that's north of Peterhead. Because at Kinnaird we couldna be sure how far we were off and then Rattray came right ahead and we had to get out a peedie bit, and the tide wasnae wrong but there was terrific seas, but we cleared it. We just had to try and do our best.

We had to do the steering, it was taking four of us at the wheel … The fireman, he fired from about six in the morning until midnight. We always usually filled the bunker for the weekend … you wouldn't say you were scared. There was work to do and you had to do it. But we had doubts about whether she would be able to make it or no. There's a heid there in Stronsay called the Brough Heid, we could see that through the haze and we just wondered whether she was going to clear it or was she no, wheeled hard over but she wouldn't answer, we finally passed by. The Stronsay men reckoned we must have gone over a skerry, we must have done, but we didna stick.

The steering chains jammed … then they went through the sheave on the deck and it was between the sheave and the big pinion wheel that the link got in and, well, it stuck so we had to get it oot and in the meantime she went broadside to the sea and she took a terrific roll and I was working the crowbar at the time, trying to get it oot. I got thrown in amongst the engine, I think it was then that the pipe to the engine snapped and so when we turned the steam on then it filled the wheelhouse with steam so we had to go onto the hand gear. There was no chance of getting it repaired. We drove a piece of wood into it to keep it tight so the steam didn't escape. It managed. I think it was better with the hand gear because if we'd had the steam gear on her it would have broken the chains, the strain was that much.

She was a good enough boat but when you came to try and drive her head-on the propeller came out of the water and she wouldn't drive but she had a good stern on her, and she would go through anything. She must have, to have survived that long.

It was just a case of try and keep her afore the wind, try and save her … We had to wait until Sunday afternoon before we got in[to Aberdeen Harbour]. There was a trawler struck the north breakwater about Hogmanay time and he sank in the channel so it didn't give you very much room to clear the breakwater and clear hid. So, they wouldny take us in and there was, I canny mind how many, trawlers and ships there [waiting to get] in. So they took them all in on the Sunday in the daylight and then took us in … we had to dodge about, there was no anchoring, all night into the afternoon. … it wasn't too bad down there because we were in the shelter of land again but there was a big sea round about …

No sleep, no food, no nothing. Just had to keep ourselves going. The steward came with a big jug o' soup and we each had a drink o' that, carry on again.

The telephones were all blown doon with the storm … but I think they got a message put through. They found oot anyway and everybody was gathering round places like the post office to see if there was any word, 'Where was she?' for they all thought she was gone. Then the word came through she was at Aberdeen. We used the signal lamp to put the message ashore to report the *Earl Thorfinn* to the Kirkwall Coastguards. They knew by this time that she was missing so they put word back to confirm the ship's name so we put the ship's name through again and that is when word got through.

We had to sort the cargo out for a start. There was a lot of perishable cargo for a start so it was just given away to the dockers and we had two bulls on board and some small pigs. At that time there was a Foot and Mouth scare on … so the only way they could do it was put them on a box and carry them through to the North of Scotland boat in the box so that they didn't touch the pier .

The steering gear was all condemned, put on new chains, new shackles. We were there for a week then we came home but we went direct to the islands to get rid of the cargo … You got the weekend off. Westray ones they had a thanksgiving service for taking us home … Everyone was thankful to see us I suppose.   *John Burgher*

Willie Mowatt had considerable experience of the Pentland Firth but was still caught out on one occasion.

I certainly got caught out once. Oh boy, in that same boat that's there. Well, I went across here from Burwick, as fine a day as this, in fact finer. A beautiful morning. I went across to Groats [John O'Groats] and I visited my relations. It blew up and I thought this was going to be a right fine sailing breeze to go home and I got the boys fill up sacks of sand for ballast, for it wasn't often to get a right fine aft of wind, a right fine stiff breeze. Got her loaded up anyhow and dammit it wasn't just a bonny-like sky but however we set off. My hell, there was a lot of people down at the pier when [we left]. We were just coming home under grand speed, to make a record passage.

It was a bloody record passage alright. Just about half way across it just came down that Pentland Firth between Hoy and Dunnet Heid, just black sky. 'My heavens' I said to the boys 'look what's coming'. I never thought ever to see the like of that on the sea. We had to take the sail off the boat and it just struck us with force and there was nothing for me but to run before the bloody lot. It was just lifting the sea out of the sea. I never thought ever to witness the like. Nothing but the bare mast on her and the sound on that mast was just like what you have heard the sound of the wind on the hydro poles. Just whining. I ran before a hell of a sea you know it was. She was just high in the air and running down the back of the lump … That boat, she just leapt in the air with the force of it, just come doon like that the wave. I had to run just fully half speed, you know. You had to run at the same speed as the lump. Faster than the lump and you would get the crest of the wave right, spilling on the top of you. At times you just felt in that lump of sea that you could come astern to climb back on the top you know … and I had a fella standing by the bilge pump to keep water out that came in … it was just what you call very careful handling … but the roar that was with that broken sea going down past you, it was a frightening sound and I saw nothing else for it but to run right east, if she would go to Norway. But I ran that much before it that I had complete confidence in that boat, how that boat behaved in such a sea and wind. I had that much confidence in her that I could run right east for the night and I ran right down surely in front of the worst dashed piece that was in the Pentland Firth.

Setting out from John O'Groats on the day of the gale

There was nothing else for it but do it. I made for the skerry. I got into skerries at the east end, at the landing and it was grand in there in the shelter … I knew quite well that that people in John O'Groats knew damn well we would never survive and the Coastguards were phoned to call out the lifeboat. I knew quite well that the lifeboat would be called because I knew that nobody thought never a boat of that size would ever survive and when we came to the skerries the sound was something terrible, about the lighthouse with the wind. When we opened the door and came on in the Keepers they just stood, stunned. They just said nothing for a blink and then says 'Where on earth have you come from' I said 'I've come from John O'Groats', and I said to the principal 'Could you be good enough to phone Duncansby and for them to contact the lifeboat station not to send the lifeboat'. He said 'That's a hell of a wind to be on the water'. I said 'Yes, but I got caught out'. Kirkpatrick told me that the lifeboat was just ready to launch when the phone rang … He says 'When I got the call at Lyness it was seventy-five mile an hour then' and I said 'It was a damn sight more where I was'.

The fellas that was with me were sitting in the bottom of the boxes and they had a camera with them too, but they were frightened to use her, it was that bad. They was watching the whole lot of it come down on top o' us but I was sitting with my back to it. The water that fell out of the lump, it was just like white suds, you know like soap and water, just roaring by ye. I don't know how the hell I ever managed to come out of it, that's the truth. But I had complete confidence in that boat. I just thought that nothing could hurt me

The funny thing was this. In bad weather, I was always at my best. I've seen on a fine day, that was the time a treacherous thing could happen, not a coarse day. I've seen me get tricked on a fine day at sea. An old fella said the same to me, it's never the coarse day you could get tricked, it's the fine one. Not wi' a gale o'wind, but with the sea.

My face was just sore for days after with being thrashed with the salt water … In the corners of the eyes here was just sore.

Were you married at the time? What did your wife think?

It was just a damn good job she was a cool person, but I expect she had her thoughts, there's no doubt about that.

Willie Mowatt

Photo: Kate Towsey

Willie Mowatt with Thomas and Allan Budge, George Rosie and Sandy Scarth at the Pentland Skerries lighthouse where they took shelter from a severe westerly

Photo: Orkney Library, Photographic Archive

BELIEF

Superstitions and beliefs connected with the sea are legion and represent ways of coping with the uncertainties of fishing and sea conditions. Commercial fishing had huge potential rewards but, in the days before fish-finding equipment, was uncertain and trawlermen were notorious for being superstitious, particularly the skippers. Superstitions vary according to generation and place of work and many are personal. Different boats can have different superstitions, although some are widespread. Some of the traditional words used to substitute taboo words survive from Norse, the language of Orkney in Mediaeval times. They have survived amongst tight-knit boat crews but died out here in general speech. Some claim that superstitions belong to a previous generation. Undoubtedly they are changing as boat crews move around more and work with people from elsewhere, but they still survive.

You learn when you go on someone's boat, if you ever mention something wrong you'll sharp find out what superstitions they [have] …   *Gary Miller*

There is a bit of superstition in everybody. Human beings simply can't get past it. They are smit with it, just the whole year round.   *Willie Mowatt*

There was very little superstition round about Westray. I never heard of that type of thing. The boys only lately have started being superstitious, since they began to take up with some of the ones from the Moray Firth. Some of the seamen now are far more superstitious than what they were when I was young.   *Thomas D. Rendall*

A lot of the old chaps were superstitious. You were'ny supposed to whistle, that was supposed to bring up wind and they never talked about rabbits or salmon, or pigs. Pigs were absolutely oot … They said about one man in particular … he'd been out west gathering a bucket o'limpets and he met the parson and he dumped them over the dyke and went home. He wouldnae go to sea with them … Some of the old seamen were very superstitious … We weren't so dependent on the weather as they had been, like, when you were under sail you were indebted to the elements, quite a bit. Superstition was quite strong … the trawlers, when they came in, you had to be very careful about what you talked about with them, they were very superstitious …   *Walter Leask*

As you leave the harbour, you turn with the sun, clockwise and you couldna speak about rabbits … they would have their own names right enough. You couldna speak about seals … no, they were a tangie wasser.   *Angus Heddle*

You don't really think you are paying much attention to it but I'll tell you one thing, I go round the shore there about nineteen times out of twenty I'll go out to somewhere I can turn round with the sun. That's when I'm driving the car. Don't ask me why.   *Alfie Sinclair*

There were certain words that were not used at sea. A pig was a cauld iron, a rabbit was a bobtail …   *Willie Groat*

You weren't allowed to say 'pig', you weren't allowed to say 'rabbits', you weren't allowed to say 'minister'. 'Salmon', you weren't allowed to say that, you weren't allowed to eat salmon. You weren't allowed to sail on a Friday but that was just to suit themselves sometimes … you weren't allowed to leave harbour on a Friday, like if it was a Friday you were leaving, you would leave it until after midnight … there was various other names for them like salmon was pink fish and rabbits was moppies and pigs was grunters and such like.   *Anon*

A lot of things couldn't get mentioned. I did anyway because it used wind the lad I was on with up. So if he pissed me off some day I just used to say a whole hash of things … he used to say 'oh that's it, we'll catch bugger all after that' and then he would catch something and I would see a smile come on his face and I would mention something else that would piss him off. Like some days you would know not to say nowt, just get on with it and say nowt.   *Gary Miller*

The younger crowd wasnae superstitious at all. I wasnae superstitious myself. I knew that thirteen is a bad number. Well I always, when I made me creels I put thirteen meshes on the eye of the creel for the lobster to get in and I was a very lucky fisherman … I never had bad luck with me creels so what the hell can you make of that?   *Willie Mowatt*

You get funny superstitions, like me, not so much superstitions. I have an undersuit and it's well past its sell-by date and a lot o' the lads are the same … you wear the same things, you don't want to change … I have this old tee-shirt that I put on over the top and it's really holey and one of the lads kills himself laughing at it because it's falling to bits but I keep putting it on … to get my gloves on I used to spit in the top and it made your hand slide in easier but like my gloves slide on easy but I still spit in it before every dive, like. You get kitted up in a certain way … I don't know if it's superstition but I wouldn't feel reet if I didna have me old tee-shirt and spit in my gloves.

Fishing, there's too many variables … I was speaking about the bits where they [clams] would be but they might not be. You might dive on a bit that they've been known to be for years and there's nothing there, why? … you just cannot put your finger on it … You get a tidal prediction book but that's all it is … they could be a lot stronger, if you've got a higher or low air pressure it can alter the tides, or the temperature of the water or the weather or if it's been windy, your visibility could be different from day to day, there's that many variables. I think the superstition creeps in to put these variables into some kind of perspective, if you know what I mean. The fellas probably know but it's better to have superstitions anyway.
Gary Miller

I can remember even in Stromness when they used to go out with the lines and that if they were heading along the street and met the minister they would just turn round and go home. They wouldn't go out that day. There was a bloke in Stromness here and he threw a rabbit's foot in his boot. He was going away to the sea and when he discovered it, it was thrown over the side but he wouldn't go out that day.
Alfie Sinclair

Superstitions about the sea didn't only concern sailors and fishermen.

We made our butter on a Saturday, the churn was taken in on a Saturday, now it was a plout kirn … the staff went up and down for about an hour. My granny wouldn't take in the kirn until it was flowing water. You didn't get good butter in an ebb tide and we knew perfectly well we could play outside while it was ebb tide, but as soon as the tide changed and there was flowing water we knew we would be called in to do something, so we had a great respect for the ebb tide.
Willie Groat

Orkney did not participate in the fervent religious revivals that characterised some fishing communities but religious observance lay happily alongside superstition.

Me grandfather had a Shetland boat and we used to make creels in the evening and go creeling in the day. We used to have seventy-five creels that we hauled by hand. Six days a week but never on a Sunday. He wasna religious, either me father or me grandfather, he would go out and sail the boat for pleasure but he wouldna go out and fish on a Sunday.
Anthony Duncan

Going out to the creels

ORKNEY AND THE SEA

Cargo coming ashore

WRECKS

Wrecks have an important place in the collective memory of the islands. Stories of ships run aground have been passed on, repeated and told so many times that it sometimes becomes difficult to gauge exactly when these wrecks took place, as tales from the eighteenth and nineteenth centuries mingle with more recent events.

Boats and ships have always run aground and, if Orcadians have played their part in rescuing survivors, there have also been times when they have been able to benefit from the wreckage of boats and their cargoes. Expert environmentalists, they are adept at recycling and re-using just about anything that might get washed ashore.

Houses may no longer be built with a cavity under the front step to conceal rescued goods, hidden from the customs men, but the drama and excitement in a good wreck tale means that it is likely to be told and re-told.

Part of a ship come ashore, Sanday

I was born in a house that was the cabin of a shipwreck and it's still there … and it was made into a dwelling house, and my father and I built the blocks round it to strengthen it for we were afraid it was going to go with the wind. It was a ship called the *Emerald* and she was wrecked at the Aikerness Holm at that place called the Quoydyke and she was loaded with barrels of paraffin … and they took her off and she was taken in below the churchyard here and auctioned … the old *Orcadia* apparently made a trip out from Kirkwall with people for the auction and they broke her up below the church here and that cabins which were forty feet long by twenty feet wide were mounted on cart wheels and towed to the north end of the island by horse and jacked up and built underneath by a old fellow called Miller, he was a boat builder … and when he got it finished he reckoned that he would of been better getting a right stone built house for this had cost him thirty pound and for another tenner he could of had a stone built house. That was 1879 when

that happened. She came in on Quoydykes in the month of November in snow showers she came ashore … and they were all saved, the dog was drowned and one of the neighbours had the collar for donkey's years …

Thomas D. Rendall, Westray

The 'Borkum' was a German ship trying to avoid capture by flying a Dutch flag. She was intercepted by the Royal Navy, who put a prize crew on board. She was attacked by a German U-boat and set on fire. She drifted ashore on Westray. The smokey grain taken from the ship was fed to hens, giving them, in turn, smokey eggs. The 'Borkum' was also credited with introducing rats to Westray.

Then there was the wreck of the German *Borkum* in the Second World War, it was in the same place the *Emerald* came at Quoydyke … and there was nobody aboard her, there was a couple of burnt corpses on her when she came ashore, it was still on fire. But there was still one or two holds of good wheat on her and they took it off her and the local men worked on it … and they took all the wheat off her and refloated her and they then took her away for scrap to Rosyth … She came ashore in November after war was declared in 1939. The one old guy that was aboard her there, he was working, filling wheat into bags and he found this nice saw in the engine room and he didn't want the customs officers see it, so he worked the whole day with it shoved down the leg of his rubber boots complaining he had a stiff leg. She lay there for about a year, there were three shell holes in the side of her.

There was one that was wrecked in the Bay of Noup I think … she came quite close in to the rocks, where she stuck and I think they more or less walked on a plank, and there was a watchman to see that no one was pilfering off her but he surely fell asleep. He wrapped himself up in a sail and fell asleep. Then some guys came on board to try to steal stuff and they picked up the sail and he came out. There was a bit of a scramble.

Anything that came ashore was fair game for anybody. That time the coal boat went ashore and the coal came ashore by the ton, and they shoveled it up off the beaches it was terrible hot stuff, it was anthracite and half of them cracked their stoves with it … far too much heat in it.

Thomas D. Rendall, Westray

I remember the *Mim*, November 1939, I think it was. … [eleven of the crew were taken off by the island's post boat on their first trip out] and stayed in the auld hut overnight. Five or six, the prize crew were taken off the ship the second time and then the engine cooling system of the post boat became blocked with debris, then Johnnie put up the sail they thought their last days had come but they made Nouster pier all right but the landing was awkward. They stayed at the lighthouse overnight and were picked up the following morning by a naval vessel off the Noust near Howar. The remainder of the crew were taken off the ship by the Stromness lifeboat and they picked up the other eleven from Nouster pier on Thursday morning. When the crew launched the ship's first lifeboat, it became unhitched before any of the crew boarded it and drifted ashore at Haskie Taing. The shattered second lifeboat came ashore in the same area on the following Sunday morning … There was a load of grain and there was a very

The *Borkum* aground off Westray

big explosion the very next night and then all the wood started to come ashore, hatches, everything, all burst like chaff of wood … It was all collected then it was given up to the receiver of wrecks and you had to pay so much to the receiver of wrecks who valued it for salvage and you claimed half. She came ashore on the Wednesday night and there was nothing left bar the funnel by the Sunday night.

Drift from the *Mim*, North Ronaldsay

Photo: Helga Tulloch

We have the second lifeboat of the *Mim* ashore. Our old trailer was made of what we believe to be the hatch off the old *Johanna Thorden*.   *John Cutt, North Ronaldsay*

They used to come ashore sometimes when it was fog. There was no foghorn or radio … If it was a foggy night they used to look forward to a ship being stranded. There was the *Geizina* came ashore, gied ashore on the Kirk Taing and the cargo was wood and they had to jettison a lot of the cargo so she could get off. It was very handy for folk making hen-houses … it was a godsend.

Jenny Tulloch, North Ronaldsay

When they blew up a blockship and I woke up one morning to see all this baulks of timber floating by the front of the house and I went to wake my father up. Father was home on leave at the time and he got up out of bed. He went to get the dinghy and this was the hatches that was blown off this ship was floating along in front of the house.

Was he able to re-use the timber?

It all went in a wooden rail round the garden, four foot high.   *Robin Duncan, Burray*

We heard about the *Lebanon* when we were rebuilding our cottage, *Bayview*, and when we were taking it apart we found that there was a beam across one of the lintels with a number carved into it and we realised that this was probably the main beam of a ship with its registration number. So we started chasing up the registration number and found that her name was the *Lebanon* and subsequent investigations showed she was built in Fraserburgh, then she went to Shetland (she was working as a fishing boat then), then she came on to Stromness and, by that time, she had turned into a sort of supply boat, a shop boat which went around the islands, then after that she was sold on to David Drever of Westray … and then she was sold on to George Nichol Rendall in Papa Westray and he ran her as a shop boat which had various crew including a man called Robbie Rendall. Then, one stormy night, she was blown from her moorings and shot across to Eday, where she was wrecked completely. So, we can only suppose at that point the crew went across to collect what they could of the remains and brought them back to Papay. It just so happened that Robbie Rendall was rebuilding a house at the time and so that's how he managed to get this piece of wood and put it in   *Tom Hughes, Papa Westray*

Everything seemed to have a history aboot the hoose. That's what it came to.   *Willie Mowatt, South Ronaldsay*

The biggest excitement was the day a boat lost its cargo out west here. The boat wasn't hurt or anything, it just lost its cargo of props and they came up on the west side, just piles and piles of them and it caused the biggest excitement that's been in Papay for a long time. Everybody had piles of props. We burnt them, just cut them and burnt them … there was about eight hundred out of one geo … we carried them up individually more or less … it was just a boat lost its deck cargo … Every available man was down there taking up props … They were too short for fencing posts but they were put to a lot of uses just the same. Some had thousands of them, those that lived near more accessible parts of the shore and could get trailers down to the shore, some just had thousands.

Greta Groat, Papa Westray

It was a treasure trove. The things you found at the shore were so unusual and, to us, valuable … we'd find things there you would never find otherwise. Pieces of wood with goose barnacles on them and we'd find tins of stuff floated off from somewhere or other and it was great fun opening it up and finding out if it was edible still and of course if a ship had gone ashore that was when beachcombing was just a pleasure … Teddy bears, teddy bears by the hundred, they would … be covered in oil and there was no way they could dry out so we emptied them of saw dust and washed them … we put fresh sawdust in them

The *Gunnaren*

and we had fresh teddy bears … all kinds of things that would float, especially tobacco … and boxes of apples. I remember we carried up cart-loads of apples from the shore and we went to the shop and got a couple of bags of sugar, just ten stone bags and we made apple jelly and apple jelly and yet more apple jelly and to this day I can't look at any more apple jelly … Apples, something we'd never seen more than one at a time. Apples galore.

Willie Groat, Longhope

I was at that wreck when I was ten year old. … I was at the shipwreck, the *Gunnaren*, a Swedish vessel … She was a general cargo; motor cars, wireless sets, everything and that one was loaded with fruit, what an amount of fruit was in that one. Apples and figs and God knows what.

Just the same went on with the *Gunnaren*. I went with my father and grandfather. There was five of us at that wreck … I was the youngest … Enormous of boats lying about that boat and stuff being lowered over the side. The customs hoose men, there was two of them aboard and what do you think a boat arrived from Stroma, just loaded wi' young boys and up the side of that ship, just like monkeys and my God, the customs hoose men couldn't keep sight of this young devils at all, but it was all the better for the other fellas … When the customs men were engaged with them for them to be looting better it was a grand cover up.

A lot went on in the dark when the customs house man was on the island. He stayed with the Rosie family on the island and he couldn't work all day and work all night. What they did, when he went to bed, the Rosie men put a light in a window to say it was all clear … and then the pirates arrived in safety and numbers.

It wasna dangerous The men knew the Pentland Firth you see and that was no danger at all. There's no great danger where there's shipwrecks, sometimes. It was the craze to get hold of stuff. It's just common sense to try and save as much as you could …

When the receiver of wrecks came round and the policeman, I think some gave up something. You know, it looked better for both sides.

When a shipwreck was on that was just it. There was some excitement then.

Stroma men was just noted pirates, but they always tried to blame the South Ronaldsay men. I mind being at that ship wreck [*Fort La Prairie*], I was at her twice, it was a great adventure. I remember there was an enormous of drink and the Stroma men got all that but if it hadna been for the Stroma men that assisted the salvage people they wouldn't have got the ship off so good. That was one good thing about them, they rode both ways.

We was a bit late getting to that wreck because they were keeping watch for pirates coming from this side going to it and me and another fella managed to go there one foggy day just sort of unknown to the Coastguards and made two trips. I mind the first trip and there was just one Stroma boat there and we climbed up the rope ladder and got aboard. The Stroma man, he said 'You've missed the cream' I says 'We know where the cream went'.

That bloody wreck too, I was not very pleased about that I got the blame for being at that ship but the boat was never off the top of the ayre. It was never launched nor nothing but this Caithness men were there and they raided her one night and a very risky business it was, with the sea and the weather that came on them that night and they left a blacksmith's hammer on the ship and this pointed at this kid … They came to find us, the powers that be, the police and that and I got interrogated here by the police and it didn't seem to matter a damn what I said as long as I proved it … I had to give my fingerprints. They were here most of the day before I did it … it was a very snidey way of doing it, for them just to leave a hammer …

It was just public talk. We knew that there was a wreck on the island of Swona and she was to be a total wreck. Natives of the islands thought that they had every right to go and help themselves when it was going to be a wreck, which was only common sense instead of seeing it go to the bottom of the ocean and that ships that came from Caithness, Stroma, Longhope, Flotta, Scapa, Burray, everywhere and this island of course …

Willie Mowatt, South Ronaldsay

This tale about the 'Pennsylvannia' comes from a Caithness man, Iain Sutherland. The John O'Groats men were half seriously referred to as pirates. There was some rivalry between them and the local South Ronaldsay, Swona and Stroma men for the cargo of any ship.

The *Pennsylvannia* … if ever you had a monument to anything in Orkney you should have had a monument to the *Pennsylvannia* … she ran ashore on Swona, I think it was 1932 or 1933. She was in general cargo … she had a'thing aboard her. She had cars, sewing machines, sparking plugs, cloth, vehicles, just aboot everything you could think o' aboard her … she was a great big boat for her day … she was six or seven thousand ton on Swona on a great storm … none o' the crew were lost, they got them all off, but a storm blew up and the customs couldn't get out to lay sight o' her cargo and the Orcadians, the Stroma men, the John O'Groats men made hay. The Stroma men managed to get two Cadillacs off her, they had sewing machines, sparking plugs and all this was in a raging storm. They had small open boats, maybe twenty feet long and they went back and fore like that … and you can be sure it was only seamen with abilities in the Pentland Firth that could have managed it. Anyone else they would have lost their life. Sheer brilliance of seamanship …

I have recordings with men from the John O'Groats side and they are aye laughing, when the storm was at its height a crew came out from Orkney in the blackness of night, to Swona. Customs was jumping up and doon trying to get out but nobody would take them out because they knew that if they took them out it would be the finish o'it because they could identify cargo and folk could then be checked up on, 'cause the customs have no sense of humour about things like that. They are aye trying to accuse folk of taking things. However, this crew came over from Orkney in the black o'night and it was pure brilliant seamanship that got them there … but they got there and they got aboard the *Pennsylvannia* in the darkness with no lights, because they couldn't show lights or the customs would see them in the dark and they took these boxes that looked promising with them, filled the boaty as muckle as they thought it would tak and went back to Orkney … when they got a look at it they found that they had risked their lives to get boxes o'shrouds

The *Pensylvannia*

and contraceptives … John O'Groats men laughed about that, in fact some of them are still laughing about that. What they could o' had and that's what they got. … You should put up a monument to the *Pennsylvania* because it made life easier for men on both sides of the Firth.   *Iain Sutherland, Caithness*

Yes, that's right and I think that happened in Caithness too. It didn't reduce the population in Orkney just the same, for as far as I knew the kids had them for balloons … At that time it must have been a privilege to have that in your possession.

The Stroma man … he came on a box o' grand silk wear … this man came home with this box and what do you think when he opened it? … it was shrouds. That was what the Stroma man got. And another man thought he was doing well with cases of rubber boots and, my god, they was all for the one foot.   *Willie Mowatt, South Ronaldsay*

She was a very old boat and she would have been well insured she dodged about, east of Sanday for two days and then fog came down and he put her ashore for the insurance would have been far more than she was worth. There was lot of sailing boats around and I suppose they just didn't pay, they were too slow beside the steam and Orkney was a grand place for them to come, there were so many tides and so many storms. The night the *Edenmore* went ashore it was dark but she had been down there twice in daylight. What for? To plot her way ashore, no doubt.

Mr Fotheringham

The *Edenmore*

The crew of the Stronsay lifeboat *John Gellately Hyndman* returning from exercise. David Rendall, Sydney Swanney, James Work snr and Willie Miller.

R E S C U E

Anyone who works with the sea learns to respect it. Knowledge of the weather, tides and sea conditions are crucial to survival. Even for the most experienced seafarer there are times when over-tiredness, unusual weather or carelessness can mean losing a ship, or worse, a life. The rescue services have always attempted to mitigate the worst effects of the sea, lighting safe paths for shipping, watching the coastline and rescuing those who get into difficulty.

Thankfully, improved contact between boats and the shore, better navigation systems and survival equipment mean that far fewer lives are lost at sea now than in previous decades. There are still, of course, risks and in many cases boats go to sea in rougher conditions and all year round. The money invested in a boat means that it cannot afford to stand idle.

Coastguard

The first life-saving apparatus in Orkney was based in Stromness in 1868. The Coastguard was divided into rescue and watchers. There were full-time Coastguards, based in Kirkwall and auxiliary watchers and rescuers, based locally. They were particularly important in the days before radio when boats had no way of calling for help should they get into difficulty. They provided a crucial service, watching and recording all marine traffic and providing the link between the other rescue services.

The Coastguard communication station in Kirkwall closed in 2000 although there are still two full-time staff, fifteen rescue teams with one hundred and twenty auxiliary Coastguards working throughout Orkney.

Jimmy Skea worked in Sanday as an auxiliary Coastguard. Helen Manson came from a family of Coastguards in South Ronaldsay and became an auxiliary herself in the 1970s. Later her daughter Anne became a watch-keeper at Brough Ness as well. Allan Taylor became an auxiliary Coastguard and then full-time, retiring from Kirkwall in 1980.

You would come on at one o'clock in the morning till seven o'clock the next night and you had no idea what was going to happen in that hours, it wasna a routine job, it wasna like working in an office when you ken roughly what was going to happen and you couldn't say 'Ach, I'll do that on Wednesday' ... you could be there just five minutes before you were due to go off your shift and someone would go ashore or shout 'Mayday' ...   *Allan Taylor*

It was bad weather watching. We were just called out when you got word from Kirkwall to set the watch. There were four of us did that. We were on about four hours, each one of us in turn. I've seen me on for three weeks, continuously. At the time that the Longhope lifeboat was lost the weather was very bad. The watch was on for more than three weeks.

There was nothing but a phone, so you could phone Kirkwall ... They kept in touch quite a lot to see what the weather was like. We had a book which you had to note down what the weather was like.   *Jimmy Skea*

You cut grass, you polished brass ... it was run as a Naval thing and every Coastguard station, if there was a war, became part of the Navy, you had an HM ship. A register that was kept in a sealed envelope and in the event of a war this envelope would have been opened and you would have kent what name you gied under like Hatston was *HMS Sparrowhawk*, the Coastguard station here would have been HMS something else, so it was all run by the Navy.

Photo: Helga Tulloch

Coastguard hut, Papa Westray

When I joined I was one of the few guys that hadna been in the Navy. I had been in the RAF before that working on air-sea rescue boats and I did a peedie bit of creeling and fishing and this kind of thing. That's how I came to be a Coastguard because I had that bit of experience. I kent which end of the boat was the sharp end and which end was the blunt end and that was it.

At that time we had a log book like what's on any ship, you kept a log, you wrote down every ship that was in the Pentland Firth during your hours of duty. You signed on the watch and you took it o'er from the other man, you then logged every ship, whether I was going east or west, what was the name of the ship or what was the number on the fishing boat. So that if there was anyone looking for it later, if they'd gone missing, at least you had a peedie record of where this boat was … You took a bearing, like what you would do on any ship's bridge, of the boat from where you were stationed and you put down the bearing … and you logged it the whole time, and if you took over a watch you read what the other Coastguard had written.

Allan Taylor

When you were on watch you were on alone, it was a bit of a responsibility right enough. When you went on watch you had to check through the binoculars, telephoned Kirkwall … everything that moved, you logged it. I thought a foggy day was the worst because you could hear ships, you knew that was a heavy engine, but you couldn't see … Also when the fishing boats, the little creel boats, had started to go off out to the Pentland Skerries and if it was a bit thick and you couldn't keep a close eye on them … that was a bit of a worry … There was no mobiles or radios or anything so they were depending on you keeping a close watch on them.

You knew everybody and where they were going and how long they should be gone up the back of the land, round the old head, or when they were getting back, you'd get a wave from them as they passed.

Helen Manson

The Pentland Firth, between the Scottish mainland and Orkney, is notorious. It has the most dangerous tide-rips, eddies and currents of any stretch of sea around the islands. A boat sailing with the tide can have as much as seven knots added to her speed or, going against the tide, can make virtually no headway.

We'd often see big ships come into the Firth at the wrong time of the tide and the tide would pull them right down, round, almost heading for the Pentland Skerries … you got in touch with the Coastguard at Kirkwall immediately

and told him the size of the ship; where she was and what appeared to be happening. It was always, or nearly always tide related … often big ships get such a shock when they come in, they stand in the face of the tide.

When they first started with the *Pentland Spray*, they towed this little *Atom* for putting people ashore, well, one day they crossed the tide at the wrong side of the Lother Rock and my father was on watch and was nearly in a panic because they were being pulled down onto the rock … well one of the men … he was brave enough to go out of the *Spray*, hand over hand into the *Atom* and manage to start the engine on that and take the weight off that. That was real panic that day. There were about fifty folk on that boat and I doubt if they knew the danger they were in.

By that time,1969, the Coastguard in Kirkwall had stopped coming down here and the Coastguards was entirely an auxiliary station, just manned by five men down here. My father was getting old and … there was a shortage of watchers. It was actually one of the Coastguards in Kirkwall who said 'Why don't you apply for the job?'. They were needing two new watchers. I said 'Me?' and he said, 'Well, you've lived here all your life, you know the coast'. My father was in a coast watch at the time, Stephen, my husband, was a coast watcher at the time and a nephew of mine and I thought, 'Well, give it a go, see what happens'.

I think they were all a bit surprised, a bit shocked in the beginning but after a week or so it was OK, they got used to it. 'A woman doing that, who does she think she is?' but why not if you could do it all?

I remember once I phoned Kirkwall and Allan Taylor was on watch and it was something that needed to be passed on to Lossiemouth because at that time Lossiemouth had an RAF station and they would send helicopters … usually that was passed through Kirkwall but he said 'You phone Lossiemouth' and I did. They didn't believe, they didn't know there were women in the Coastguards. Very much surprised voice on the other end on the phone saying 'Oh, we weren't aware there were lady Coastguards'.

Women weren't supposed to do a night watch. They weren't supposed to watch after twelve o'clock, as if that's different to one o'clock …

The Coastguard has gone and the people from the lighthouses have gone so if there is anything unusual, there's nobody reported … ships would lose deck cargo and things like that that must go unreported now.

Helen Manson

[In the event of a distress call] you took all the initial action, you would call out the Coastguard rescue company, you called out a lifeboat … and after that you told the boss what you had done and let him worry about it.

A rescue exercise in Stromness harbour using the lifeboat and helicopter

Searching was the main thing, there's not an island on Orkney that I've not walked around or been to, even the peedie uninhabited ones, looking for someone. Most of the time there was no radios on peedie fishing boats and if it came fog you were looking for them and things like that. It was just grand when you found them but when you didn't find them it was a different kettle of fish.

You had a kit bag beside your bed you had your torch, oilskins, rubber boots, tobacco tin, everything in it and you would get a ring at three o'clock in the morning … the guy that was on duty used to ring the bell and of course every Coastguard house had a bell and if you got one ring of the bell you would go down to the duty room and two bells meant that you had better get your gear all on and three bells meant just grab your bag and don't ask questions that was it. You could've been going anywhere out on a boat or anything.

… you called out a lifeboat, you had to keep contact with it. The first thing you did was you laid out a chart … and you would then plot your lifeboat and the ship it was going to, so you could kent the wind speed and direction and you could do an 'interception', this is when the one boat would go past the other. You could guess, well, it was more than a guess. It was what you were trained to do with navigation, to get the wind speed, direction and speed of your lifeboat which of course you kent because you were probably talking to him but with the other ship, if it was a foreign ship and it was drifting and it was a light ship obviously she would drift far faster than a heavily laden ship … You had this estimated out then, or if there was an on shore wind and it was drifting to shore you would have a Coastguard rescue company standing on the beach with breeches buoy … and you had a thing they called a guard of the station. Every fortnight you walked four miles on each side of your station and every second fortnight you walked eight miles. You had to walk that bit of the beach so you kent every nook and cranny and the man at the next station had to do the same. All right round Britain. Local knowledge was the prime thing.

The first thing we got was radios, VHF radios there was about twenty-four batteries in them and they weighed about half a hundredweight and the batteries didna last. They were pretty hopeless. If there was a hill or a house in the middle of it you couldn't get a clear signal. A big Marconi set stood in every Coastguard station, we had one of them but then they were fiddly things, your aerial tuners and everything … Latterly everything was recorded, twenty-four hour a day in the station. Every ship that's talked to you, every telephone call. Like the man that's sitting there on watch, if he was to order a pound of mince from the butcher it would all be on tape … In the case of an emergency this court inquiries deaths but in me days a guy would take your log book and put a bit of red tape on and seal it and then he took it away.

During the training everyone had to go out to a life-raft launch a life-raft, and sit in a life-raft and be rescued by a helicopter and landed back at the station. This was because if you were speaking to a guy on a ship and telling him what to do you had already gone through this experience.

I suppose it was a worry for the families, but me family grew up with it like … the Coastguard service owned you at that time because you lived in their house, you couldna be a Coastguard without living in official quarters … When you went on holidays you had to leave the key of the house in the duty room in case of a fire. If your granny or anyone came to visit you had to tell them who it was, under the Official Secrets Act in case they were communists and was going to blow you up.

It didn't matter who you were looking for, they were somebody's son or husband.

Local fishing boats was your main work when you had good communication between the North Isles and the South Isles, all the boats were running back and fore you could speak to them and say 'Have you seen so and so?' and if it there was anything to be seen in the Flow at all they would have seen it. This was in the days of VHF radio, it was a brilliant invention because it was a just peedie box that everyone had set in. You could phone your granny and tell her to get your tea on that you would be there at half past six … which is really brilliant. It's saved many a life.

The worst thing for anybody at sea or the Coastguard was fire and fog … fog you couldn't see where you were going until you got radar. Ships was lost … they would lie off for hours and hours … and there was no echo-sounders or nothing, it was just a steering wheel and a compass and what you had learned all your life … if you kent what the whitemaas was saying about the craigs you kent whether you were off Copinsay or coming in to Shapinsay, that kind of thing … I mind a guy from Stronsay going ashore on a foggy night, he walked up to a phone box to find out where he was and then gied back on his ship and shouted 'Mayday' …

I mind a man I still work with at the Red Cross saving me life once. At that time a life-raft came in at one of the Barriers and to find out what ship the life-raft was from you needed a label from the bottom of the life-raft with a number … and I was going to go down, it was a bad kind of day and at that time we had duffel coats like you see on old Navy pictures. He reckoned that I would be better with a life-line on going down and I was glad that he had mentioned it because I got washed right down and I never seen the colour of the water.

You don't need a Coastguard station here now, I suppose. You could run it from the moon because technology has advanced that far.

Allan Taylor

Lifeboats

Lifeboat men and women are respected as a symbol of concern for the lives of others. The lifeboats put to sea in conditions when no other boat would consider setting out, at great risk to lives of the crew. Orkney has an honourable tradition of supporting the lifeboats. There has never been a shortage of volunteers to crew the lifeboats or to support them in their work.

Stromness Lifeboat Station, established in 1867, covers the north and west of the islands. Longhope Station was established in 1874 and covers the Pentland Firth, along with the Wick and Scrabster boats. Stronsay Lifeboat Station was open between 1909 and 1915 and then again between 1952 and 1972 and covered the North Isles, then Kirkwall Lifeboat Station was opened in 1972, covering the North Isles and the Pentland Firth.

As with the Coastguard there are often family traditions of joining the crew of the lifeboat with generations of the same family connected to the same station. Like the Coastguard, this tradition also now extends to women.

Angus Heddle was part of the Longhope shore crew and his daughter is now part of the crew of the Longhope boat. William Sinclair was Coxwain of the Kirkwall lifeboat and Alfie Sinclair was Coxswain of the Stromness lifeboat.

Photo: Orkney Library Photographic Archive

Lifeboat being launched, Stromness

I remember her being launched. We'd see the rocket and then we'd all run along. We liked to see her go into the sea.

Walter Leask

When we left school we used to go doon there when the boat geid oot and work on the slip, launching and hauling up ... I'd have been nearly sixteen ... Anytime the boat gied oot you just gied doon to see what was going on so I think you just got involved that way. My brother, he was the Winchman at that time so I used to go along with him sometimes ...

Angus Heddle,

When I was about two three years old I would go down [to the lifeboat shed] and watch my father. He was the Winchman, launching the lifeboat and pulling the boat up after exercise. I used to go down with him just about any time, see what was going on ... I just stood at the back of dad, watching what they were doing. Then I started working down there when I was fourteen or fifteen working with ropes and stuff then. Once I was eighteen I went on the lifeboat then.

Lorna Heddle

Crew of the Kirkwall lifeboat at a presentation to Magnus Work for long service

She [my daughter] used to come down when she was peedie ... when she came to an age when she could join the crew she just joined. I think she just prefers the sea to the land.

Angus Heddle

You were just a decky, working with ropes again but at sea ... they just asked me, probably because I had been hanging around for years ... I knew a lot because of just being there since I was small, just telling you bits when you were younger and showing you round, so I knew most of it already. Then when you were on the boat just being shown.

When you're out there you are more or less just concentrating on what you're doing. Right enough, when you come back you sometimes think, well maybe it was rough but when you're out there you never think about it.

Lorna Heddle

It just stayed in sort of a cradle and she stayed level in the cradle and you cart the cradle doon to the door you knocked the pin out and she sets off down the slip then. Latterly they didn't work with the cradle. I suppose it was more for the petrol engines in the old boat that she stood level in the shed the whole time.

They put off maroons at that time, two maroons and when you heard them you went down. There was no phone in

them days ... we just used to run over the fields. No cars in them days. I didn't even have a push bike. The Secretary used to get the word from the Coastguard and phone the Coxswain and it was old Bob who used to let off the maroons. They could tell then where they were going ... The first thing the crew did was put on their oilskins and while they were doing that, the shore crew were getting the doors open and getting the engines started, by that time they had their oilskins on and you just got them oot as quick as you could, you know.

We used to go home and listen to the wireless. In them days you could listen to them on the trawler waveband, you ken. You could listen in on the wireless and ken what was going on. You'd know then when they [the lifeboat] were coming back and the Coastguard would send a message to the Secretary to let you ken when they were coming back in ... You'd to put the ropes down each side and take the big cable down the slip. It depended on what like the conditions were, if they were bad, if there was an inshore wind sometimes they couldn't land her and had to go back to the pier and wait until conditions improved. Sometimes she'd lie there for days before they could get her back up the slip.

A radio and a compass was about all the boat had when I first went down and the radio just wasn't all that dependable, the aerial gave trouble sometimes.

They didn't have the navigation that they have now and it was quite common for trawlers to go aground, bigger ships too.

Angus Heddle

… you worked together … we maybe say 'Shall we cut up through here?' and he would say 'Yes that's a good bit'. I knew quite a lot of it but you didn't know everything but you had someone who had lived up in the Isles and they knew a lot better which way to go.

I think we were far enough away from Poole [RNLI Head Office] that nobody bothered us too much up here. You weren't on the mainland. You were always a bit of a problem to get here.

They [employers] were quite happy that you did it. Most places you would find that there was never any problem with that. You quite often find that the Harbour Master is the Coxswain of the lifeboat.

William Sinclair

The helicopters have made life an awful lot easier for the lifeboats. The only place a helicopter cannot go is under the face of a very high cliff but the boys in the helicopters are really good on their jobs.

If you were Coxswain then you were stuck up in the wheelhouse so the Mechanic did all the talking on the wireless.

Alfie Sinclair

In Orkney you've quite a long way to go. If you got a call up from the North Isles, say north of Westray, ten miles north of the Noup Head, that would take you three hours to get there and three hours back. That's six hours steaming right away. That's quite unusual for lifeboats to do. Normal lifeboat stations are close together … they are only twenty, thirty miles apart.

Most of our work on the lifeboat was in the wintertime, when it was foggy you know. We did quite a lot of searching in Orkney, you know someone would report a red flare and you would go and you would spend all night maybe up round the

North Isles or something. Nine times out of ten there was nothing there, but you had to go.

The new types of boats are faster. The one we had, the *Grace Paterson Ritchie,* was only twelve knots and then the new boats they were doing about, and the ones now do even more, twenty-six knots, I think and you have to be young and fit to go in them. They crash about so much … you have seat belts, you never had that … the *Grace Paterson Ritchie* had one seat, the only seat available was for the Mechanics … there was accommodation down below, with just bench seating.

The older boats, there was no radar, no proper echo-sounder. A heck of a lot of it was just guessing where you were going and they just basically the older lifeboats just had compass and a wireless. The echo-sounders weren't up to much really, they were quite good but no like now.

If you called up a fishing boat and said 'could you give us a hand searching?'. Oh yes they would always stop and have a look.

William Sinclair

People knew they were certainly taking a risk going out in such a small boat but they took in their stride, just part of life, you know.

You miss it, yes, it fine to go down there for a yarn with the boys. You ken what was going on better when you went down there.

Angus Heddle

I suppose about twenty or thirty years ago. You always had so many of them, you had Lossiemouth but you never had the dedicated helicopters but they are using them more and more now … it was only when the North Sea oil started that they started coming in …

William Sinclair

For Orkney, the worst disaster at sea was when the Longhope lifeboat (the 'T.G.B.') was lost with all eight crew in 1969 while going to the aid of the 'Irene'. Helen Manson's father and her husband were Coastguards on duty that night in South Ronaldsay where the 'Irene' went ashore. Angus Heddle was part of the lifeboat shore crew in Longhope. William Sinclair was on the Kirkwall lifeboat which also came to assist and then search.

I mind us coming round the Mull Head, off Deerness there, we had a lot of sea there that night. The [Kirkwall] lifeboat fell there. I reckon she fell about seventy or eighty feet, the length of the lifeboat … she just went over the top of a wave and there was nothing there, she just fell down with a crash.

William Sinclair

The *T.G.B.* lifeboat on exercise

If you hadn't seen the seas that night you couldn't imagine, just high above the land.

That night of the Longhope lifeboat, it was such a tragedy. The *Irene* was a Greek ship and she was light, she was going to go from Granton to Norway and she got caught up in horrendous, horrendous seas, terrible easterly winds had been blowing for a whole week and she got caught up in that up the east side here. Stephen and I were just coming out of the byre when we saw the red flare and it was absolutely horrendous so we phoned the Coastguard immediately … that must have been like half six in the evening and of course the coast rescue services were called out. That meant everybody that was young and fit had to go out, heading along the coast, keeping an eye on this ship to see where she would come ashore, or whatever else might happen. My father, he went on watch, must have been about seven o'clock that evening and just stayed on overnight and of course when she came ashore, near to the Grimness shore it was just as though she had parked herself, she just came right in, I think a big wave threw her over on the side there but she just sat there, down below the shore, by the time she actually landed the men were there with their rescue equipment.

They fired a rocket over the *Irene* very quickly, they couldn't get, you are talking through loud hailers, that kind of thing and they couldn't get the Greek men to understand to pull this light rope … that one was lost … somebody came over the side of the ship so there was a bit of a hoo-ha going on … someone came down from Kirkwall and the Deerness men arrived as well, to help. It was the third rocket … By that time they were pulling the men ashore and the Deerness men arrived.

They took seventeen men off of that ship and it was such a wonderful rescue and they were on such a high about that … but … it the meantime of course the Longhope lifeboat had been launched and it was only when she came oot between Brough Ness and the Lother, tremendous seas there and she wouldn't have known up in Longhope, just how bad the sea was in the Pentland Firth. She knew it was bad but she wouldn't have known how horribly bad and my father was on watch and there is a place called the Lother Head, very, very bad and she got through that and he thought 'Gosh, if she gets through there she'll get through anything', but then, just about nine o'clock she was towards the east of the Pentland Firth to a position half a mile south of the Lother Rock that she encountered the flood tide ease and he just saw her lights disappear there and och, he was just heartbroken, absolutely. I spoke to him maybe half an hour later on the phone and he said 'Brave little boat, brave little boat', I can hear him still, saying that 'But', he said ' She's gone'. He never saw the lights again.

They were all men that he knew and respected for what brave seamen they were. That blighted everything … the rescue was such a high it was great to save all these men but … Everybody was in mourning, every house in the place. It was as if you had thrown a blanket over the place … Nobody knew what to do or what to say … it devastated everybody …

As so often happens after these things a week, ten days of bad weather, it was a calm day the day after. Strange …

The rescue was still going on, besides, it was dark and of course a lot of people were hoping that she had got round the corner, she was maybe just out at sea, you know, all the things that you hope for, this kind of thing, you know in your heart … the search didn't start until the next day but before that you had a whole night of silence. Everybody knew to expect the worst …
Helen Manson

… they had what was a rescue shield which was a silver shield which was presented every year to the Coastguard station that had done the best, the last time it came here it was after the Longhope lifeboat was lost because they took seventeen of a crew off the *Irene*. That was probably the longest watch I ever did. I gied on duty at seven p.m. and I was still there at seven p.m. the next night the whole time, just myself, my head was just pounding … we were looking for the Longhope lifeboat and I ken every body that was on it. I was the last body to ever speak to them, well at that time the only person they were speaking to was the Coastguard and the only Coastguard was me … It was one of the saddest occasions. We were all sort of high that night because the boys had rescued seventeen off this Liberian ship but then by one o'clock we still thought the Longhope boat would turn up the next day but it was turned upside down in the middle of the Pentland Firth.
Allan Taylor

I remember the whole thing. It was a rough night and it had been strong winds for days and days before you know, a gale going on for a long while it just seemed to ease, the wind gied doon. She just geed oot as normal and there was nothing different. She lost radio contact but we didna think much o 'it, it was quite common for the radio to go off anyway with the aerial in bad weather but then it was next morning there must have been something wrong because nobody had heard from her. Especially when they had never turned up to the scene with the Kirkwall boat … I ken them all, been to school with a lot o'them.

They were searching all around and the Thurso boat actually found it, overturned … they took her to Scrabster and upturned her. She was never back here again … When they took the coffins back we met them at the pier at Longhope … The ones that volunteered to make up another crew right away. I suppose what maybe made it worse that night was they were going in between South Ronaldsay and the skerries, right in the tide rip and it being dark you couldn't see anything coming at you.
Angus Heddle

Photo: Orkney Library Photographic Archive

Lighthouse staff being taken off by breeches bouy

Lighthouses

The lighthouses around Orkney are crucial to the safety of shipping. Orkney has eleven major lighthouses and eleven minor lighthouses in addition to eight unlit beacons and twenty-one buoys. The first lighthouse was built in 1789 in North Ronaldsay and the last, in Copinsay, was lit in 1915. Since the 1960s the lighthouses have become automated and are now all un-staffed, maintained by local Assistant Keepers or by visits from the 'Pole Star', the Lighthouse Board's ship. The last Orkney lighthouse Keeper in North Ronaldsay left his post in 1994, after this light having been continuously staffed for more than 200 years.

The Lighthouse Service had many similarities with the armed services with uniforms and ranks. Lighthouse Keepers were regularly moved around between different lighthouses. North Ronaldsay, Noup Head, Pentland Skerries, Auskerry, Helliar Holm, Cantick Head, Start Point, Graemsay and Copinsay originally had family living-quarters where the families of the lighthouse Keeper would stay. Sule Skerry was staffed by one Keeper and two Assistant Keepers who were moved around on six month shifts (more frequently in later years). Supply boats were meant to visit regularly but, in bad weather, it could be up to six weeks between boats and the Keepers would see no one but each other. Many Orcadians have served as occasional Keepers, helping the regular Keepers with maintenance duties and watches. Some went into the Lighthouse Service itself and worked around Scotland.

Each year when they came around they asked us where we would like to be sent to next. I said I wanted to work at any out of the way family station where I could take my family, as opposed to a rock station. Lo and behold we ended up in North Ronaldsay.

Quite often ships in trouble don't say they are really in trouble until the last minute and by then it could be too late. The Braer oil disaster happened near Sumburgh Head and I think quite honestly if there had been a Keeper at Sumburgh Head that night, I think they would have seen a ship in trouble, probably long before it radioed its distress signal.
Jimmy Craigie

The mothers or the wives used to be able to contact [at the rock stations] them on the radio so they would speak to their husbands.
Frank Davidson

[We had to] assist maintaining the lighthouse, night and day. With a paintbrush and a scraper, basically. Oh, digging trenches, every outside thing was painted once a year, more or less regardless. The lens had to be kept spotless. The whole thing had to be kept clean, brasswork polished. It looked nice ... You had to wind the machine periodically throughout the night. You would be up and down the tower through the night winding up the machine that made the light revolve. You've always got to keep an eye out for fog and if the visibility dropped down below four miles you'd start up engines that drove compressors for the foghorn.

I love being away at remote places ... I like being away on the extremes of things you know. It's great being up in the middle of the night and maybe keeping an eye on a whole area of coastline, it's only you keeping an eye out everywhere ... keeping an ear open for the radio ... great feeling.
Jimmy Craigie

I must have been eighteen or nineteen when I cam back as occasional Keeper at Copinsay, let men off on holiday. It was a good enough paid job but it was only eight or nine weeks in the year .... There wasn't many bairns there but after the school came to be at the island there was a few Keepers that came with bairns .... Barra Head it was a most ungodly spot on the earth, the nearest shop was sixteen miles way by sea. Copinsay was a good thing compared with it. At Barra Head there's no living folk near you. Uninhabited island ... and there's a big boat that came out every week in the summer and every fortnight in the winter. I've seen the boat ten days late on top of the fortnight and you are starting to get hungry then.

When I was there [Copinsay], there were three great big engines there, flywheels about five or six feet in diameter and they were old-fashioned oil engines and they were damned things to work. You had to heat them up with a blowlamp and you'd get them to start and then you got them going, chuff, chuff and when they were running right, they wasnae fast, every now and again if they got too hot they gave off a hell of a bang. If they were going too slow, or too cold there'd be another dirty old bang come out of

Copinsay lighthouse

them. Some explosions coming off that things. There went along with the paraffin into that engine a wee tank with a wee spigot and if you got too much water it would bang. If you got too little it got too hot there was another big bang. They were damned things. You didn't need to be an engineer to drive them you needed to be a magician. They were made before they were invented.   *Jimmy Groat*

It [Papa Stronsay] was only a minor light but it used to be painted once a year. They had railings right around it and he used to put one of us boys on the outside and one of us on the inside so we could paint the whole things in one go … they had a gun to put on, a gas operated gun for drifters coming in in fog … they used to depend on hearing the gun. Quite often this plaguing thing didna work in fog because dampness seemed to spoil it.   *Jack Scott, Papa Stronsay*

It was generally keeping the light in order, cleaning the lens, paint the outside, changing the mantles, and winding up the clocks … It was all doubled up. If one clock failed then the other one would still work the light. Everything was doubled up. Gas was used to revolve the light and supply the gas to the light. The only thing the clocks did was switch the gas on and off …

It will be the engineers from Edinburgh that will deal with it from now on, just fly up in a helicopter. It's the biggest

change in the Lighthouse Service is the helicopter. Before, when the engineers came, they had to stay maybe two nights on the island. Stay the night, walk across and work the day then go back again. The helicopter has done away with all that, they can fly in any time they want. If there is a fault on it at all it registers in Edinburgh and they just fly up. Other than keeping it clean I don't think I'll have anything to do with it.

It's kind of hairy coming up the stairs at night when the light's no lit up you always think you can hear something, echoes of your own footsteps I suppose.

The flash sequences is different on every light. This flashes two white every twenty seconds. This light has the black and white stripes for daylight navigation. Every tower is slightly different.   *Andrew Skea, Sanday*

From my early days in the job the automation programme was in swing and they were picking away at them here and there, and you knew the end was coming as it were and eventually it did come.

As you were sent from lighthouse to lighthouse they were working at the automation process at every place I worked. That did get me down … I feel sad, going back there it is like a ghost town. It will never be our lighthouse again.
    Jimmy Craigie

Cleaning the glass

The lighthouse maintenance ship *Pole Star*

The 'Pole Star', the Lighthouse Service ship, is based in Stromness and has had many Orcadians serving on it.

I mind I joined on, I think it was a Wednesday and Thursday she was sailing out to Sule Skerry to do the reliefs then it was to be back into Stromness and back off to the Flannans ... do the relief there and then back to Stromness. I stayed the Wednesday night on the ship ... I'll never forget off Cape Wrath that night it was about a westerly force eight and me being Ordinary Seaman, my room was way down in the bottom of the boat and there was a porthole and when she was diving into the sea the water was up to the porthole and I thought 'Good God what am I doing here?' and we got out to the Flannans and did the reliefs there and, sod's law, on the way back it was a westerly. I thought when we get back that's it. To me Cape Wrath is a place that I hold in awe, it is very rough there. It was there I thought 'You either make the sea your career or you get away from it' and I think it was that time I thought 'Right this will be what gives me a living for the rest of me life'.   *Willie Tulloch*

When I joined the only day you got off was Sunday and if there was an emergency you went off just the same and when I joined it I got ten days holidays a year. *John McIvor*

Brass was the great thing. I mind when I was on deck on the *Pole Star* ... Friday afternoons, scrub the deck and polish the brass. Then, if it rained, all the polish was a waste of time.   *Willie Tulloch*

You were away from home quite a lot. You were away practically the whole summer, down the west coast overhauling the lights right down to Oban. Some of them did go home for weekends but I never did.

We had to make sure that all the lighthouses that we visited were topped up with gas, cylinders of gas that kept the light working and in addition to that there might be painting to do. They get a bit tatty with being exposed to the elements.

You had to paint all the unattended ones ... all the way from here to Oban.   *Frank Davidson*

On the first boat there was no cabins at all, there was just an open room and the beds on one side and a long table in the middle and you had to carry your own food and cook your own food ... and I'm telling you some of it was gey strong in that hot weather you'd get in the summertime ... there was no refrigeration ... you got fourteen days' supply, your teas for fourteen days, it was getting gey strong by the time your fourteen days were up and you got near a shop to get fresh supplies.

All the lights were paraffin and you landed the year's supply in the summer, and it lasted you the whole year. It was forty-five gallon barrels and some of the lighthouses didn't have a pier or a slipway or anything to land them on so you had to dump them over the side of the boat and roll them up over the rocks and by the time you got them up to the station the damn things got square. It was tough going.

They were difficult things to get at ... Start Point was about the worst round here.   *John McIvor*

The crew of the lighthouse maintenance ship the *Pole Star*

Photo: Orkney Library Photographic Archive

Not all rescues are performed by the uniformed services and many Orcadians have assisted vessels in difficulty on their own initiative and assisted the rescue services.

When I was a boy, just have been in the cradle, a drifter came ashore on Papa Stronsay, a very rough night, and they took a boat ... and rescued the crew ... it was before my day of knowing things but my dad said I must have known something was wrong because I howled and better howled most of the night. *Jack Scott*

We just happened to see a flare and we couldn't get him on the radio and I said to the boys 'We'd better go back and see what happened'. So, when we came in he was sort of lying on his side and no very good condition at all but we eventually got a rope on him and got him pulled out. There were nobody lost but they were very lucky all the same. We got him towed out, in the shelter anyway and got him straightened up and towed him home.

We took a man off a trawler in Westray one time who got burned and we took him to hospital in Kirkwall. It was actually a bit dodgy coming alongside the trawler, they more or less just threw him down. He survived anyway. Any other rescues we did, it was generally just go alongside and pick anything up but you were often called out with someone sighting flares. It was a common thing.

Jimmy Stout, Stronsay

The seamanship there is incredible because we are going where other ships should not be going. You're lifting buoys. In the old days you were going into the lighthouses although now it's done by helicopters ...

What gives you a lot of satisfaction is if it is a bad night you have to concentrate to navigate. I always find if I can put the ship alongside the pier without a bump, then great satisfaction. *Willie Tulloch*

Now, of course there is no one on any of the lights. No Grace Darlings to rescue you. *Frank Davidson*

It was a community within a community. We used to do Sule Skerry, Swona, Pentland Skerries, Flannans, but I mind Auskerry being manned, Noup Head, North Ronaldsay. But it was marvellous. I've seen us putting stores ashore at Sule Skerry and it would take us the whole day. I used to come in with the boat and, once they got themselves sorted out, I used to go up to the light and have a blether with the Keepers and it was just like long-lost friends and now it seems lonely because all the lighthouses you go around and nobody is there but you can remember the laughs you used to have there with the light Keepers. *Willie Tulloch*

Papa Westray heroes; William Hume and Andrew Groat awarded medals by the King and the Royal Humane Society for bravery at the wreck of the *SS City of Lincoln*, September 30, 1905.

Photo: Orkney Library Photographic Archive

Willie Groat, Papa Westray

Alex Costie

Thomas B. Rendall

Oliver Scott

Jenny Tulloch

Meg Fiddler

George Drever

Greta Groat

Willie and Jim Work

Harcus Scott

Jimmy Stout

CONTRIBUTORS

Where possible dates of birth have been given.

Cyril Annal, born 1945. Interviewed in Burray by Alexander Annal
John Burgher, interviewed in Kirkwall by Kate Towsey
Alex Costie, born 1949. Interviewed in Westray by Helga Tulloch
Geordie Costie, interviewed in Westray by Helga Tulloch
Jimmy Craigie, born 1949. Interviewed in North Ronaldsay by Helga Tulloch
John Cutt, born 1956. Interviewed in North Ronaldsay by Helga Tulloch
Frank Davidson, born 1922. Interviewed in Shapinsay by Ellen Casey and Helen Chalmers
John Davidson, interviewed in Shapinsay by Ellen Casey and Helen Chalmers
Robin Dennison, interviewed in Shapinsay by Ellen Casey and Helen Chalmers
George Drever, interviewed in Westray by Helga Tulloch
John P. Drever, interviewed in Westray by Helga Tulloch
Anthony Duncan, born 1939. Interviewed in Burray by Kate Towsey
Robin Duncan, born 1935. Interviewed in Burray by Alexander Annal and Kate Towsey
Meg Fiddler, interviewed in Stronsay by Helga Tulloch
Mr Fotheringham, courtesy of BBC Radio Orkney
Julie Gibson, interviewed in Rousay by Kate Towsey
Edwin Groat, interviewed in Westray by Helga Tulloch
Greta Groat, born 1926. Interviewed in Westray by Helga Tulloch
Jimmy Groat, born 1911. Interviewed in Deerness by Jenny Ireland and Kate Towsey
Willie Groat, (Papa Westray) born 1922. Interviewed in Westray by Helga Tulloch
Willie Groat, (Longhope) born 1919. Interviewed in Longhope by Kate Towsey
Jock Harcus, born 1911. Interviewed in Kirkwall by Calum Robertson
Angus Heddle, born 1934. Interviewed in Hoy by Kate Towsey
Lorna Heddle, interviewed on the *Hoy Head* by Kate Towsey
Marcus Hewison, interviewed in Westray by Helga Tulloch
Tom Hughes, interviewed in Papa Westray by Helga Tulloch
Walter Leask, interviewed in Stromness by Helen Chalmers and Kate Towsey
John McIvor, born 1923. Interviewed in Shapinsay by Helen Chalmers and Ellen Casey
Helen Manson, born 1937. Interviewed in South Ronaldsay by Kate Towsey
Gary Miller, born 1963. Interviewed in South Ronaldsay by Kate Towsey
Mungo Montgomery, born 1945. Interviewed in Burray by Alexander Annal
Willie Mowatt, interviewed in South Ronaldsay by Kate Towsey
Willie Muir, born 1923. Interviewed in North Ronaldsay by Helga Tulloch
Thomas B. Rendall, interviewed in Westray by Helga Tulloch
Thomas D. Rendall, interviewed in Westray by Helga Tulloch
Sandy Robertson, born 1908. Courtesy of The Royal Commission for Ancient and Historical Monuments
Malcolm Ross, born 1912. Interviewed in Flotta by Calum Robertson
Harcus Scott, interviewed in Westray by Helga Tulloch
Ian Scott, born 1940. Interviewed in North Ronaldsay by Helga Tulloch
John (Jack) Scott, born 1921. Interviewed in Kirkwall by Kate Towsey
Oliver Scott, born 1936. Interviewed in North Ronaldsay by Helga Tulloch
Alfie Sinclair, interviewed in Stromness by Kate Towsey
William Sinclair, born 1935. Interviewed in St Mary's by Kate Towsey
Andrew Skea, interviewed in Start Point Lighthouse in Sanday by Calum Robertson
Jimmy Skea, born 1916. Interviewed in Sanday by Calum Robertson
Jimmy Stout, interviewed in Stronsay by Helga Tulloch
Iain Sutherland, courtesy of BBC Radio Orkney
Robbie Sutherland, born 1924. Interviewed in Stromness by Kate Towsey. Part prose and part transcription
Allan Taylor, born 1929. Interviewed in Kirkwall by Calum Robertson
Jenny Tulloch, born 1920. Interviewed in North Ronaldsay by Helga Tulloch
Willie Tulloch, born 1950. Interviewed in Stromness by Helga Tulloch
Jimmy Wilson, Born 1925. Interviewed in Sanday by Calum Robertson and Kate Towsey
James Work, interviewed in Stronsay by Helga Tulloch

Willie Muir

Thomas D. Rendall

Jack Scott

aak	common guillemot
bannocks	flat bread made with oatmeal or bere
bushel	volume of about 35 litres
clam	scallop
cuithes	coalfish in its second year
cruisie lamp	small, open oil lamp
dan	float used by divers to mark their position in the water
Decca	a system of long ranged navigation developed by Decca Co in 1946
drouger/druger	large boat, strongly built, designed to take animals to a large vessel
duff	plum duff
dunter	eider duck
dyke	wall
fathom	normally six feet, but sometimes taken as the span of out-stretched arms
flattie	small, flat-bottomed boat popular particularly in Stromness. Square stern and a pointed bow, built with a tongue and groove bottom and clinker-built sides. First built in Stromness in 1890s, initially used as a fishing boat.
flit	to move house
foy	party
geo	sea inlet
hid	it
kelp	the ashes of seaweed used especially as a source of iodine
kist	box
leapid/leepid	scalded
partan	edible crab
phlense	remove the skin from a whale
piltick	coalfish in its second year
pund	enclosure for animals
pram	small boat common to North Ronaldsay
raffle	muddle
ro-ro	roll-on, roll-off; ferries which vehicles can be driven on and off
Sankey hymns	hymns written or collected by the American evangelist Ira Sankey who toured Britain in the late nineteenth century
sillocks	coalfish in its first year
skarf	the cormorant or the shag
skrek	high pitched yell
spoots	razor fish
steethe	foundation of a hay stack
swapping	catching auks by sweeping a net before them
tang	seaweed that grows above the low water mark
ton	the imperial ton equivalent to 1016 kilograms
ware	seaweed that grows below the low water mark
Westray skiff	double ended sail boat common in Westray. Originated in the early 1800s used for inshore fishing. Keel length between 15 and 20 feet.
whitemaas	gulls
yole	double ended, clinker-built sail/rowing boat. Variations within the design all over Orkney dependent on local building traditions and local sea conditions eg. South Isles yole had two sprit sails and a jib whereas the North Isles yole would have two standing lug sails and a jib.

BIBLIOGRAPHY

Butcher, D., *Following the Fishing*, Tops'l books, 1987

Cormack, Alastair and Anne, *Days of the Steam 'Earls'*, The Orkney View, 1990

Dickson, Neil, *An Island Shore: selected writings of Robert Rendall*, Orkney Press, 1990

Fenton, A., *The Northern Isles: Orkney and Shetland*, J. Donald, 1978

Ferguson, D.M., *Shipwrecks of Orkney and Shetland and Pentland Firth*, David and Charles, 1988

Gibson, W. M., *The Herring Fishing, Stronsay Vol. 1,* B.P.P., 1984

Gunn, Neil M., *The Silver Darlings,* Faber and Faber, 1941

Lockhart, G.W., *The Scots and their Fish*, Birlinn, 1997

Martin, Angus, *Fishing and Whaling*, National Museums of Scotland, 1995

McRobb, Alastair W., *The North Boats*, Ferry Publications

McRobb, Alastair W., *The Second St Ola*, Thuleprint, 1977

Miller, James, *Salt in the Blood: Scotland's Fishing Communities Past and Present*, Cannongate, 1999

Miller, James, *Wild and Open Sea, The Story of the Pentland Firth*, The Orkney Press, 1994

Morris, Jeff, *The History of the Stromness Lifeboats,* Coventry, 1999

Oral History Society, The Journal of the Oral History Society c/o Department of Sociology, University Essex, Colchester, Essex

Stromness Museum, *'For Those in Peril': Orkney Lifeboat History*, Stromness Museum, 1977

Stromness Museum, *Sail and Steam*, Stromness Museum

Tanner, Matthew, *Scottish Fishing Boats,* Shire Publications, 1996

Thompson, P., *Living the Fishing*, Routledge and Kegan Paul, 1983

Thompson, Paul, *The Voice of the Past, Oxford University Press, 2nd* edition 1988

Thomson, William P. L., *Kelp-Making in Orkney*, The Orkney Press, 1983

Thomson, William P. L., *The New History of Orkney,* Mercat Press, 2001

Wilson, Bryce, *The Lighthouses of Orkney*, Stromness Museum, 1995

But, John, have you seen the world, said he,
Trains and tramcars and sixty-seaters,
Cities in lands across the sea -
Giotto's tower and the dome of St. Peter's?

No, but I've seen the arc of the earth,
From the Birsay shore, like the edge of a planet,
And the lifeboat plunge through the Pentland Firth
To a cosmic tide with the men that man it.

Angle of Vision, Robert Rendall

Yet the sun shines doun on a' thing,
The links are bonny and green,
An' the sea keeps ebban an' flowan
As though it had never been.

from *Cragsman's Widow* by Robert Rendall